W9-BIH-069

Date: 2/9/17

FIC GREGORY
Gregory, David,
Open : get ready for the
adventure of a lifetime /

Open

Open

GET READY
FOR THE ADVENTURE
OF A LIFETIME

DAVID GREGORY

Tyndale House Publishers, Inc.
Carol Stream, Illinois

Visit Tyndale online at www.tyndale.com.

TYNDALE and Tyndale's quill logo are registered trademarks of Tyndale House Publishers, Inc.

Open: Get Ready for the Adventure of a Lifetime

Designed by Jennifer Phelps

The author is represented by Chip MacGregor of MacGregor Literary Inc., PO Box 1316, Manzanita, OR 97130.

Library of Congress Cataloging-in-Publication Data

Names: Gregory, David, date, author.
Title: Open : get ready for the adventure of a lifetime / David Gregory.
Description: Carol Stream, IL : Tyndale House Publishers, Inc., 2016.
Identifiers: LCCN 2016021340 | ISBN 9781496413963 (hardcover)
Subjects: LCSH: Bible. Gospels—History of Biblical events—Fiction. | Jesus
    Christ—Fiction. | Christian life—Fiction. | GSAFD: Christian fiction.
Classification: LCC PS3607.R4884 O64 2016 | DDC 813/.6—dc23
    LC record available at https://lccn.loc.gov/2016021340

Printed in the United States of America

22	21	20	19	18	17	16
7	6	5	4	3	2	1

To Trinity,
our family's true writer

ONE

IT WASN'T THE END of the world. It was only the end of *my* world.

My girlfriends all said the usual things:

"You'll be better off without him."
"There are more fish in the sea."
"He doesn't know what he's passing up."

My journal recorded all the usual pep talk:

"I'll learn from this and become a better person."
"I wasn't ready to get married yet anyway."
"This will give me a chance to focus on my
    career."

I wasn't buying any of it. The truth was, I had made a huge mistake. I'd broken up with the best guy I'd

1

ever met. Jason and I had been together for almost two years. My whole future was tied to him. Or so I thought—until he came to my North Dallas apartment one evening after a third job interview with the same company, full of excitement.

"Well?" I asked as I opened the door.

Jason took me into his arms and kissed me passionately. "I accepted the position!"

"You did!" I kissed him back. "That's fantastic! When do you start?"

"Next week."

"Wow. That's quick. At which office—downtown or Galleria?"

Jason took a deep breath and sat down on the couch. "Well, neither."

I kept standing. "What do you mean, neither?"

"They want me to go through their management training program."

"Which is where?"

"Atlanta."

I dreaded asking the next question. "For how long?"

He hesitated. "A year."

* * *

Jason moved to Atlanta. We called each other. We e-mailed. We skyped. And after three months, we broke up.

I was the one who did it. I was always the one who did it, breaking up. I just never thought I'd do it with Jason. If I had to explain it, I'd say I never got over the feeling that I was second place to Jason's career aspirations. I knew his career was important. But couldn't he pursue a career within driving distance of me? If I had been the most important thing in his life, he wouldn't have moved away for a year. I couldn't shake that feeling, no matter how often I told myself it wasn't forever.

So on a fateful Friday night, facing another lonely weekend, I called him and said straight out, "Jason, I can't do this anymore. It's over."

He didn't have much of a reaction. That should have told me something. He certainly didn't plead with me to reconsider.

I lasted two weeks without him. No phone calls. No e-mails. No skyping. And I was miserable. Wherever I fell in Jason's priorities, I missed him horribly. I finally swallowed enough of my pride to call.

"Hey, it's me."

"Hey. I'm surprised you called." His tone seemed distant. Not that I could blame him.

"Yeah. Well . . ." I took a deep breath. "Jason, I made a big mistake. I was being emotional. I was feeling rejected, like I wasn't important to you anymore. But I love you, and I know you love me, and I think we can make this work out. I'll move to Atlanta if I need to—get a job doing whatever."

There was silence on the other end.

"Jason?"

"Yeah."

"Did you hear what I said?"

"Yeah."

"What do you think?"

He didn't respond. A knot formed in my stomach.

"Jason, I'm sorry—"

"Emma . . ."

"What?"

"I met someone at work."

*   *   *

A month later, I opened my apartment door just after six on a Friday night, changed out of my work clothes, turned on the TV, and looked through what was on. News. Sports. The *17 Again* movie. *I wish I was seventeen again*, I thought. *And I'm only twenty-nine.*

I kept looking. Kids' programming. *Wheel of Fortune. Property Brothers.* I settled for *Property Brothers.*

That pretty much summed up my life—*settling*. Instead of pursuing better jobs elsewhere, as Jason had, I had settled for a mediocre job just to be close to him. Instead of remaining near my social group, I had settled for a new apartment close to work but an hour away from all my friends. Instead of staying at the great church I had attended for ten years near my old place, I had settled for a church down the street where I didn't know anyone. I had settled for a life unlike everything I had expected even six months before, and I felt like I was going nowhere.

I reached over to the end table next to the couch and picked up my Bible. I'd been reading it more frequently since Jason and I broke up. Not that I never read it before that, but I'd mostly let my relationship with God coast during my time with Jason. I went to church, participated in the career group, listened to Christian radio in the car, and tried to catch time for praying and Bible reading when I could, but I didn't spend much time alone with God. Now, I had all the time in the world for him.

My real question was, did he have time for me? Because, to be honest, I wasn't feeling him all that much. The Bible was supposed to guide me. Comfort me. Reassure me. Wasn't it? But as I opened it for the umpteenth time since Jason and I broke up, my expectations couldn't have been lower.

God, I found myself praying—or thinking, at least; I'm not sure it was officially a prayer—*I don't feel like I'm getting anything at all from the Bible. What good is reading these stories from the Gospels? None of them has anything to do with what I'm dealing with right now.*

God was supposed to satisfy me. Isn't that what all the Christian music said, or implied? And that's what I'd been told over and over by every youth pastor, college pastor, normal pastor, abnormal pastor, whatever—let God himself satisfy you.

The only problem was, sitting on my couch alone, reading stories in the Gospel of John that I'd read a thousand (okay, numerous) times, it just wasn't true. Jesus *wasn't* enough. The Bible *didn't* provide the answers I needed. I hated to admit it, but it felt like my only real fulfillment was in the past. He'd moved to Georgia four months before.

But it wasn't just my lack of fulfillment that concerned me. For the first time since high school, I found little doubts about my faith starting to creep into my mind. At first I dismissed them. *Everyone has doubts from time to time*, I told myself. But the thoughts kept reappearing, troubling me. "You can't judge God's existence based on the circumstances of your life," I had heard at church. But that was all I had to go on. All my life I had been taught about God's goodness and love. But where was his love when something happened that really mattered?

To be honest, these thoughts frightened me. I had never been one to doubt my faith. What if I couldn't shake them? I didn't want to live the rest of my life not even knowing whether God existed.

I sighed deeply, put my Bible on the coffee table, and grabbed an ice cream sandwich from the freezer. I walked out of my apartment to the mailboxes. Maybe there'd be an interesting insurance company letter in my box. I pulled out my mail and glanced at it. A pile of ads. A dental office coupon that looked like a credit card. An oil change coupon. An insurance letter (I was right!). Two letters that looked like credit card applications. And a greeting card with my name and address handwritten on the envelope. *Huh.* Despite my momentary hope, the handwriting wasn't Jason's. And it didn't have a return address. On the back of the envelope was written one word in ornate lettering: *Open.*

I wanted to open it right away, but it would have been awkward with my ice cream sandwich, so I walked back to the apartment and put everything down first.

Who could have sent me a greeting card? I tore open the envelope. On the front of the card was a picture of a sunrise shining through a tree with words I recognized:

"And now these three remain: faith, hope and love."

1 CORINTHIANS 13:13

Someone was sending me spiritual encouragement. That was nice. I opened the card to see who had sent it. On the inside I found handwriting that matched the envelope. It said simply:

For a real adventure with Jesus, go through the nearest open door.

No signature. No name at all.

For a real adventure with Jesus. What did that mean? Who in the world would have written me such a mysterious note?

I glanced at the envelope again. No further clues. I looked over the card again. Nothing. A friend must have sent it, although I couldn't imagine who.

The odd thing—and all of this was odd, really—was that the sender was encouraging me to walk through the nearest open door. What did that refer to? I thought about it. What were the doors God had opened in my life right now? I picked up a pen from the table and started a list on the back of the envelope.

Interview at accounting firm

After taking my current job, I'd been asked back for a second interview at an accounting firm in town. I'd declined it, but they left the door open, saying they'd like to talk if I changed my mind. The job I'd taken wasn't turning out all that great. Maybe going for a second interview wasn't a bad idea.

Fall mission trip

The career group at my new church was taking a short-term mission trip to Honduras in the fall. I'd have to ask for vacation time I hadn't officially earned yet, but maybe going on the trip would be good for me. It would be a good way to get to know people in the group better. And mission trips were supposed to be life changing. *I could use some positive life change at this point.*

Michael

A guy at church had asked me out. I'd told him no. The last thing I needed was to jump into another relationship. But maybe I was wrong. Maybe moving on was exactly what I needed.

That was about it—all the open doors I was aware of. Except my friend Allison had invited me to move in with her. Did moving back across town constitute an open door? And did I want to commute to work an hour each way just so I could be closer to my friends? I jotted it down anyway, just in case.

Allison's apartment

I looked at the note again.

For a real adventure with Jesus, go through the nearest open door.

An adventure with Jesus. Did that mean the mission trip? That was the most Jesus-oriented door in front of me. Maybe God would direct me—although, to be honest, I was never really sure about his direction in anything.

I wandered back to the living room and glanced at my Bible by the couch. Maybe that was the open door: spending more time with Jesus in his Word. That's what Christians are supposed to do, isn't it? I sat on the couch and opened the Bible again, this time to somewhere in the Gospel of Mark. I started reading:

> That day when evening came, he said to his
> disciples, "Let us go over to the other side."
> Leaving the crowd behind, they took him along,
> just as he was, in the boat. There were also other
> boats with him. A furious squall came up, and
> the waves broke over the boat, so that it was
> nearly swamped. Jesus was in the stern, sleeping

on a cushion. The disciples woke him and said to him, "Teacher, don't you care if we drown?"

He got up, rebuked the wind and said to the waves, "Quiet! Be still!" Then the wind died down and it was completely calm.

He said to his disciples, "Why are you so afraid? Do you still have no faith?"

They were terrified and asked each other, "Who is this? Even the wind and the waves obey him!"

The story was great, miraculous. But how in the world were these Bible stories in any way relevant to my life in the twenty-first century?

I stood up and walked to the bookcase. Maybe there was something here I could actually get into. The Narnia series. I'd loved those when I was younger. Maybe I'd enjoy reading them again. A bunch of books on Christian living. A lot of good *those* had done me. Several interior design books my folks had given me back when I had thought about changing my major. One of them caught my eye: *Doors*. It was a coffee-table book, almost too big for the bookcase. It was about . . . doors. All kinds of doors. Large. Small. Fancy. Plain. Ancient. Newly made. Not the most practical book, but I liked it. I liked the idea of doors, opening to new rooms, new houses, new possibilities.

And then a silly thought struck me. What if the greeting card was referring to a literal door? What if I was literally supposed to walk through the open door closest to me?

I did a quick glance around the apartment. The closest door led to my bedroom. And it was open. Feeling utterly ridiculous, I walked through it. On the other side, I discovered . . . my unmade bed, clothes on the floor, and two boxes of books I'd never unpacked.

Well, so much for walking through a literal doorway. I glanced at the clock. 6:23. It was still early enough to go out and do something. Maybe go to a movie. I think I even had a box of candy in the pantry to take with me. I walked toward the pantry door, which stood slightly ajar. Then I realized I'd been mistaken. When I opened the card, my bedroom door wasn't the closest open door. The pantry door was.

I instinctively glanced around me to make sure no one was watching. I pushed the pantry door wide open. The pantry wasn't exactly big, but I could actually step inside if I wanted to. Maybe my next adventure with Jesus involved the Cheez-Its on the shelf to the left. I stepped through the pantry doorway.

That's when the first wave smacked me in the face.

TWO

I GASPED FOR AIR. *What—*

My hands reached to clear my eyes. Too late. Another wave smacked me from the back, almost pushing me off the seat I occupied. *What in the—*

I heard voices—clamoring, panicked. I could feel water all around my feet. No, at my ankles. *What am I doing in a boat with water in it? Am I dreaming?*

I took a look around me. I was on a bench in a boat. Ten or so men, shabbily half-dressed, were frantically trying to keep it afloat. Four were rowing. The others were bailing water.

This can't possibly be real. This can't *be real. I would never even get into a boat like this.*

The boat rocked wildly as waves pummeled us. The men's shouting was barely audible over the wind, rain, and waves.

Real or not, I have to figure out what's going on here.

Although it was daytime, I could barely see beyond the edge of the boat. Whether we were ten feet from shore or ten miles, I had no way of knowing. I only knew two things for sure. First, we weren't in the ocean—I didn't taste a lick of salt as another wave hit my face. Second, the men's efforts to save us all were clearly failing. I could feel the water creeping up toward my calves.

I grabbed on to the side of the boat behind me and clung tightly. As I did, one of the men near me turned toward the back of the boat and shouted.

"Master!"

I looked in the direction he was facing. Who was he shouting at?

"Master!"

Another wave hit me. With one hand I pushed the hair away from my face and cleared my eyes. Then I saw him—three feet away from me, a man sleeping under a blanket on a cushion at the rear of the boat. *How can anyone—*

The shouting man staggered past me to the figure on the cushion. *Doesn't he notice that a woman has suddenly appeared on his boat?* He shook the figure and screamed, "Master, don't you care if we drown?"

Wait. This seems familiar.

And then a truly bizarre thought occurred to me: *Is this my adventure with Jesus? Have I . . . have I been somehow transported into this Bible scene? Is that even possible?*

The sleeping man awoke, moved the blanket to the side, and stood, steadying himself with his hand on the boat's side. He looked to be thirty or so, in good shape, average height. He was dripping wet. He stepped past me and looked out over the water.

He opened his mouth to speak.

That's when the biggest wave hit me. It broke over my head, completely engulfing me. I fell backward with the wave, grabbing with all my strength to hold on to the side of the boat.

But the boat was gone. I was by myself in the raging water.

I flailed wildly, trying to pull myself to the surface. My head finally broke into the air. I wasn't drowning— for the moment. But I was still being buffeted by waves that swept over me every few seconds. When my head bobbed above the water, I tried to see the boat. But the rain was coming down so hard and the daylight was so dim that I couldn't make out anything. I forced myself to think.

Be calm, Emma. Jesus is quieting the storm. In a minute this lake will be like a sea of glass, and then maybe he'll reach out and pull you out of the water, just like he did when Peter sank.

But seconds passed. Many seconds. A minute. The

storm didn't subside. Neither did the panic that began to well up inside me.

I really am alone. And I don't think I'm dreaming. I'm on my own in this storm.

I'll have to swim for it.

The good news was that I swam competitively in high school. The bad news was that I wasn't in nearly the shape I'd been in twelve years before. The really bad news was that I had no idea what direction land lay in—or how far away it was.

My panic told me to just start swimming in any direction as fast as I could. I had to get to land. Now. My logic told me the opposite. I quickly kicked off my tennis shoes. I straightened out, flipped on my back, and, trying to take breaths in between the waves engulfing my head, I started to backstroke. However far I was from shore, my best chance of getting there was to backstroke.

I swam. I gagged on water. I tried to keep my head above the surface. Minute after minute after minute. The remaining daylight slowly vanished. I was in utter darkness. I had no idea what was ahead or behind me.

I simply swam. My arms and legs ached. *Keep going, Emma.* They ached more. *Keep going.* They started throbbing. *Keep going!* They screamed at me that I could not swim another meter. *I can't go on! I can't go on!* But I did.

My left arm scraped hard against something. I dropped my feet and touched what felt like the lake bottom. I tried to stand on wobbly legs, then collapsed back into the water. I stood and stumbled forward in the darkness. Five steps and I had escaped the water.

Where I was, though, I had no idea. I never knew darkness could be *this* dark. There was no way I was going to take a step away from this spot. For all I knew, in another hundred feet I could walk over a cliff. I'd just have to wait until daylight.

I sat down on the muddy beach. Two seconds later a voice jerked me to my feet.

"You're safe with me." It was a man's voice.

I didn't know whether to be terrified or relieved. I strained to see who was speaking to me, but it was hopeless. I couldn't see anything.

"Who are you?" I asked apprehensively.

"I'm the Lord of the storms."

I heard him sit down in the mud. The rain had stopped. All I could hear was my labored breathing and waves from the lake lapping gently at my feet.

A thousand things came to my mind. One seemed of paramount importance.

"Am I really here?"

"You are."

"I mean, I'm not dreaming?"

"No."

I could feel the goose bumps rise on my arms in the dark. I wasn't sure whether to be excited or terrified.

"But how did I get here?" I asked as I sat back down.

"We brought you."

"We?"

"My Father and I and the Spirit."

"But how is that possible?"

"My Father exists outside the realm of time."

I had the feeling I wasn't going to get much more explanation than that. I decided to switch to the second topic on my mind.

"You didn't calm the storm," I said, half-accusingly. "Why didn't you calm the storm?"

"It's calm now," he replied.

"But I almost drowned!"

"No, you didn't."

"I should have drowned."

"You couldn't make that swim yourself, but I was giving you all the strength you needed."

We sat for a moment in silence. Couldn't he have done more than supply me strength—like pull me out of the water?

"I did just what you told me to. I walked through the open door."

"Yes."

"And I found myself right in the middle of a storm."

"Yes."

"So why didn't you calm it right away?"

"Why would I have done that?"

"Because that's how the story goes—you calm the storm."

"Emma, I *sent* the storm. Why would I want to calm it before it had accomplished its purpose?"

I let that sink in. I'd done exactly what Jesus told me to do, and look where it got me. He didn't just send me into a situation that turned out to be difficult; he brought me to a place he *designed* to be difficult—life-threatening, in fact. What did this say about Jesus?

"I'm not sure I can trust you," I finally said.

"You can trust me," he replied.

That was all he said. No further explanation. No promises. Nothing.

"I'm not sure I want to trust you."

"Well, that's up to you, isn't it?"

I heard Jesus get to his feet and start to walk away.

"You're leaving?"

"I have to be somewhere," he replied.

"Am I supposed to follow you?"

"You're supposed to meet me."

"Where?"

"Not where. When."

"How am I supposed to meet you?"

"Walk straight away from the beach up the hill. At

the top you'll see morning breaking over a village. Go there and walk through an open door."

His footfalls got farther away. In a couple of minutes, I'd lose the option of following him.

I stood up. "And what if I just want to go home?"

His voice was no longer close. "Just say, 'I want to go home.'"

I hesitated and then asked one last question. "But what will I miss if I do that?"

I could barely hear him now. "The answer to your question."

I could feel my brow crease. "What question?"

I waited for a response, but he was too far away.

"What question?" I shouted.

I stood still and listened. All I heard were the waves lapping at my feet.

THREE

I CROSSED THE BEACH AND started walking up the hill. "Ow! Ohhh!"

I bent down and picked a prickle out of my right foot. As I did, my arm scraped against something sharp. "Ow!" I held my arm close to my face to check it out. I still couldn't see a thing.

Great. I'm climbing a hill in bare feet, stepping on prickles and scraping against bristly bushes. The words *I want to go home* formed in my mind. I chased them away. Whatever Jesus had planned for me—I guess I just assumed it was Jesus I'd been talking to. Who else could it have been? *Maybe I should have asked him, just to clarify.* Anyway, whatever Jesus had planned for me, surely it was worth stepping on a few prickles. At least jeans were protecting my legs.

Five minutes and only two prickles later, I reached the top of the short hill. The first rays of sunlight were breaking over the horizon. Below me, maybe a ten-minute walk away, lay a small village. I was about to head in its direction when a thought occurred to me.

What are these first-century people going to do if a woman in a T-shirt and jeans, and soaking wet, walks into town? Don't they have laws about women wearing what they would consider men's clothing?

And then a truly chilling thought struck me.

Didn't they stone women for that sort of thing?

The last instructions I got from Jesus almost ended up drowning me. I wasn't at all sure I wanted to follow these new ones.

I looked down at my jeans and saw two items by my feet, barely visible in the still-dim light.

Sandals. And, from the look of it, just about my size. I slipped them onto my feet—a perfect fit.

Jesus had left me a pair of sandals to walk in. Would he do that and then have me get stoned? Surely not. *Almost* surely. I decided the risk was worth taking. I started down the hill.

A few minutes later, I approached the edge of the village. How was I possibly going to blend in? Then I remembered: I didn't need to blend in. All I needed was an open door. If I attracted hostile attention, I would simply dash for the nearest open door.

I got within maybe fifty yards of a short, adobe-looking structure when the first threat emerged.

Several houses down, a man came around a corner and turned my way, leading a mule. *He's walking straight for me.*

I stopped. I was too far from the buildings to out-run this guy. I wasn't going to try to dash past him. I glanced behind me. I was probably too far from the hill to outrun him to the top. I was trapped.

I stood and simply waited. *Jesus, I could use your help here* was all I could think.

The man and his mule came closer. I braced for flight. Suddenly a rooster let loose a loud crow. I almost jumped out of my skin but forced my mouth to stay shut. The man didn't change his pace. He had to be within fifteen yards. My muscles tensed. Ten yards. He didn't glance up. Five. Nothing.

He passed right by me.

I stood there, speechless. And then I remembered: the men on the boat hadn't seemed to see me either. Was I invisible to everyone except Jesus? And even he hadn't exactly seen me; when he'd been with me, it was pitch dark. I looked toward the town. Maybe this place wasn't such a threat after all.

Slowly, I made my way into the village. With day-break, people were beginning to stir. I heard a few random voices and more roosters. A woman wearing a head covering and a veil over her face emerged from a house, a young child following her. She left the door to the house open as she and the child turned into an adjacent covered area. *A stable?* I heard animals making noises—goats, maybe. I looked again toward the door. Hopefully, if I went through it, it would lead somewhere else. If not, I'd simply be barging into a first-century Hebrew house for no reason at all.

I glanced up and down the street. I saw two more women, both with covered heads and veiled faces. They weren't looking in my direction. I walked briskly toward the doorway that the first woman had emerged from and glanced inside. Three children were still asleep on straw mats. An old woman lay next to them, snoring. Even if anyone *could* see me, this was probably as good a chance as I'd get to try this undetected. I took a deep breath and walked through the doorway.

* * *

I squinted at the bright sunshine. The early morning had immediately given way to a sun directly overhead. The lake and hills with vegetation had given way to a brown, dusty landscape. I could see a village in the distance. It looked bigger than the one I had just passed through. On the other side of the village stood some large, brown hills. To my left were smaller ones with what looked like caves in them. The sudden scenery change wasn't as jarring as it had been the first time. Maybe I was getting used to traveling this way.

In front of me, fifty yards off, a man was sitting by himself on what looked like a small stone wall. He motioned toward me. I looked behind me and then back toward him. *Is he signaling me?*

"Emma!" I heard him shout in my direction. As far as I knew, there was only one person in this century who knew my name.

I walked toward him. I was about to shout back at him, "What question?" But as the words formed on my lips, I saw a figure walking our way from the village. It was a woman, by herself, carrying what looked like a large water jug. Something about her didn't seem quite right. I couldn't put my finger on it.

I paused, and then it occurred to me that this woman wouldn't be able to see me any more than anyone else in this century had been able to. Except Jesus. I walked closer to the two of them.

For the first time I got a good look at him. Slightly dark skin with an olive tone. Black hair. Dark brown eyes. His height, as far as I could tell, was pretty average. Unlike many of the portraits I had seen of him as a kid, he appeared . . . Jewish. Very ordinary looking.

The woman came to where Jesus was sitting, by what I could now tell was a water well. Suddenly I realized: *This is the woman at the well.* I was about to witness one of Jesus' most famous encounters.

Without looking at Jesus, the woman put her pot

down next to the well and started to lower a bucket. I moved closer and took a better look at her. She looked worn down by life. Her forehead was lined with troubles, her face drawn by anxiety. Her clothes were dyed red and yellow, not the plain, off-white clothes I had noticed in the previous village. They were tattered at the edges, as if the woman wanted to dress nicely but no longer had the money to keep up the appearance.

And then what didn't seem quite right struck me: she wasn't wearing a veil, or even a head covering. The women I had seen in the other village wore both. All the women in this culture probably did. This woman looked like she had given up even trying to play by her society's rules.

"Give me a drink, please," Jesus said to her.

The woman stopped lowering the bucket and stared incredulously at him. "What did you say, sir?"

"Would you give me a drink?" he repeated.

She pulled the bucket back up, filled with water, and then turned to Jesus. "How can you, a Jew, ask me, a Samaritan woman, for a drink?" She paused. "Is that really what you want?"

It took a moment for her words to sink in, but they did sink in. She was a woman, out here alone. A promiscuous woman, as I recalled from the story. He was a man, alone. Men didn't approach women like this here. *Does she think he's propositioning her?*

Jesus ignored her question. "If you knew what God was offering as a gift, and if you knew who at this very moment is asking for a drink, you would ask me, and I would give you fresh, living water."

She glanced at the well and then back at Jesus. "This well is really deep, and you didn't bring anything to draw water with. Where are you going to get fresh water? Jacob, our ancestor, gave us this well. He and his sons and his cattle drank from it. You're not greater than he was, are you?"

Jesus stood up and emptied the bucket into the woman's pot. "You drink this water, and how long does it quench your thirst?"

"What do you mean?" she asked.

"When will you need to get more?"

"Tomorrow."

He nodded. "Of course. You drink this kind of water, and you will thirst again. But I'm offering a different kind of water. Whoever drinks of my water will never thirst again. My water becomes like a spring of water on the inside of you. It never stops flowing."

The woman knelt down before him. "Sir, give me your water. That way I won't be thirsty, and I won't have to come down here every day to draw from this well."

Jesus put the bucket down next to the well and turned to the woman. "Why don't you go get your husband? Then come back, and we'll talk some more."

The woman's eyes drifted to the ground. "I don't have a husband."

Jesus sat back down on the stone wall. "That's true. You've had five husbands, and the man you're with now isn't even your husband."

The woman's eyes shot up and met Jesus'. She was clearly taken aback by what she had just heard. "It's obvious you're a prophet," she said, redirecting the conversation away from herself. "Our fathers worshiped here, on that mountain." She pointed to the large hill on the other side of the village. "But you Jews say that people have to worship in Jerusalem. So which is it?"

Jesus leaned toward her. "I'll tell you a secret. God isn't bound to one place, and he doesn't care if people worship him on this mountain anymore. And he doesn't care if they go to Jerusalem to worship him. From now on, true worshipers will worship the Father wherever they are. They will worship him through a new spirit he will give them. This will be the truest part of them now, that they are joined to him. These are the worshipers the Father looks for. God is Spirit. To worship him truthfully, you have to be one with him in your spirit."

The woman looked confused, and she picked up her pot as if she were about to go. "I know that the Messiah is coming. When he gets here, he'll tell us everything we need to know."

Jesus stood up next to the well. "Woman, you are speaking with him right now."

The woman started to respond and then heard something behind her. I glanced up and saw a group of a dozen or so men—exactly a dozen, actually—walking toward us. They were dressed in simple, light brown clothes. *The disciples.* I had seen them in the boat, of course, but it had been too dark to get a good look at them. Right now, they seemed as incredulous as the woman had when Jesus first spoke to her, scandalized that Jesus was conversing with a woman alone.

The woman got up, left her water pot by the well, and ran back into the village.

One of the disciples held out some bread that they must have bought in town. "Teacher," he said, "have something to eat."

Jesus shook his head. "I have food to eat. You just don't know about it."

I heard a couple of the men ask those standing next to them, "*You* didn't bring him anything, did you? Who brought him food?"

Jesus smiled. "This is my food: to do the will of the one who sent me and to accomplish his work."

He stepped toward me and nodded with his head toward one of the shorter hills. "I'll be back shortly," he said to the disciples as he walked away. I followed him.

"What question?" I asked him when we were out of earshot of the disciples.

"You don't remember?"

I searched my memory. "No."

"You will."

We got to the bottom of the hill and started the climb. "So tell me," he said, "what did you think of that woman?"

"The one at the well?"

"Yes."

I had read the story of Jesus and the woman at the well before—probably a dozen times. I decided to answer honestly. "I think I don't relate to her very well."

He looked over at me but kept walking up the hill. "Really? Why not?"

"Because of who she is."

"And who is she?"

"She's a first-century peasant, which I can't relate to. She's been married five times, which I'll never relate to. And now she's living with a man, which I certainly can't relate to. I can't believe she can even get away with that in this society."

Jesus smiled and kept walking up the hill.

"What?" I asked.

He took several more steps and didn't respond.

"Why are you smiling?"

"Because of what I know, but you do not yet."

I stopped where I was and crossed my arms. "Which is what?"

He looked back at me. "That woman is exactly you, Emma."

FOUR

JESUS STARTED BACK UP THE HILL.

"Wait a minute!" I called after him.

But he kept going until he got to the top. I arrived there two minutes later, breathing heavily. Jesus was already sitting on the ground. I stood, hands on my knees, catching my breath.

"What do you mean, I'm just like her? I'm not like her at all."

"I beg to differ."

"Okay," I sighed. "How?"

"Have a seat," he said.

I sat on the ground and looked out over the valley below. The brown landscape was interrupted by several small groves of trees and some patches of crops. Far to the left I could see an ocean. My geography wasn't the best, but at least I knew where Israel was. *That must be the Mediterranean Sea.* In the distance on my right a much greener stretch of land extended away from us, where a river likely ran through.

Over the years the thought had occurred to me that one day I would like to visit Israel, to see where Jesus walked. Now it was all laid out before me. *This is where Jesus walked. Or rather, walks.* I stole a glance at the man sitting three or four feet from me. It still seemed unreal. *How can I possibly be sitting here next to Jesus?* Despite my momentary irritation at his words, I could see why people idealized the experience of the disciples, actually being beside him every day. I wondered how, after this, I would ever adjust to my life back in Dallas.

"Okay," I said, my soul much quieter now. "Tell me how I'm like that woman. I don't get it."

He picked a rock off the ground and turned it over slowly in his hand. "She's been let down by life. She had high hopes for finding the right answer for herself, and nothing has worked. Relationships have let her down. She's given herself to six different men. Five rejected her. Now one takes advantage of her. That's a lifetime's worth of rejection." He looked at me. "Have relationships let you down, Emma?"

I nodded. Even two thousand years and ten thousand miles away from home, it seemed like I never stopped thinking about Jason. One would think that the incredible series of events I'd been dragged into would have taken my mind off him, but it hadn't. Even sitting on a hill with the Savior of the world, I still wanted Jason. What did that say about me?

Jesus picked up another rock and looked it over. "Friendships have let the woman down. In fact, she doesn't have any friends, and she feels all alone. That's why she was out here at the well by herself and not with the other women. The women in town won't associate with her. They're afraid she'll steal their husbands." He put the rock down and looked at me again. "Do you have close friends, Emma?"

"I have close friends," I replied defensively, and then paused. "But not really to be with anymore. I moved away from them." I looked down at the village below. "I guess people don't move away from their friends and family much in this kind of place."

"No, they don't."

We sat silently for a few moments, looking out over the valley, and then Jesus spoke again. "There's one other thing that's let her down."

"What?"

"Religion."

"Because she's a Samaritan?"

He shook his head. "Because she's human. Religion always lets people down."

That was the last thing I ever expected Jesus to say.

"She's confused," he continued. "She has a religious

system she's grown up with, but she knows there's something more. That something comes through the Jews, who despise her because she's a Samaritan. The Jews are constantly putting her people down. So it's all confusing to her."

He turned toward me. "Let me ask you a question, Emma. Has religion let you down? Has the Christianity you've embraced lived up to all that was promised?"

There wasn't much point in denying the truth. "No. Not really."

I figured we were about to launch into a discussion about the shortcomings of twenty-first century Christianity. Or, worse, a discussion about what I needed to do to make God a higher priority in my life. But he asked, "So, if you were counseling the woman, what would you say she needs?"

I shrugged.

"What would you say?" he repeated.

I ran my fingers through my hair. It was a mess. I hadn't brushed it since I had almost drowned in the Sea of Galilee. "Well," I breathed deeply. "She could use a man who would really love her."

"Yes."

"And she could use a close friend or two, which she doesn't seem to have."

"Yes, and what else? What would you tell her if she lived in your time and place?"

"I guess I'd invite her to church, to one that hopefully would love and accept her and teach her the truth about God. Maybe get her into a good women's Bible study or discipleship group."

"Good. Now she has a loving, committed man, good friends, and a good church. So let me ask you this, Emma. Has she found what she's looking for?"

I started to open my mouth, and he held up his hand. "Before you answer," he said, "I'd like you to meet one more person."

"Who?"

"You'll see."

He stood and started walking down the hill. I followed him. I looked toward the well down below. People were walking to it from the village.

"Where are we going?" I asked. I tried to keep up with his pace. It seemed as if he walked up and down hills like this all the time.

"I'm heading back to the well."

"What for?"

"To meet with the men from the town. She went back and told them there was a man at the well who knew everything she's ever done. The men are worried. They want to know if 'everything' includes any details about them."

"What about me?" I asked.

"You can move on to your next appointment."

"Last time you sent me into the village to find an open door."

"That was a test. You don't really need more open doors now that you're here."

I stopped on the hillside. "A test? A test of what?"

He stopped and looked back at me. "A test of whether you would do what I told you to do."

"But . . . I thought you knew everything. Didn't you know what I would do?"

He smiled. "It wasn't to show me what you would do. It was to show you."

* * *

The scenery changed. The gentle, grassy, sloping hills of Galilee and the dusty plains of Samaria had given way to a rocky, cliff-filled wilderness. It was hard to believe anyone would choose to inhabit this land, but ahead of me, maybe a hundred yards off, a crowd had gathered. I didn't have much doubt who was in the middle of it.

I walked up and saw Jesus giving hugs and blessings to small children. Their parents hovered, beaming. Jesus' disciples stood aside looking glum. Why were they looking so downcast?

I looked behind me and saw scores more people—maybe hundreds—with their children. Word had clearly spread. Whatever plans the disciples were counting on for the day were doubtless shot. I couldn't help but smile. No wonder they were unhappy. They were trapped in the middle of nowhere watching Jesus bless a never-ending stream of children.

I watched as Jesus hugged and laid his hands on and blessed each child. He was sitting on a large rock, and kids were climbing all over the rocks behind him. People were arriving from every direction. It was a madhouse. In the midst of it, Jesus seemed perfectly content to take time with each child, one by one.

After a while, I found a rock to sit on and watch. The blessings continued until the sun started to set. Jesus finally dismissed the crowd. He and the disciples headed west down the road. I followed. From that direction, casting long shadows, a procession approached. Four burly men were carrying a solitary figure in a decorated carriage. He wore a finely woven, bright white cloak with purple and gold trim and a headdress studded with jewels. He was young— twenty, maybe. The men carrying him were armed with swords, as was an entourage of perhaps a dozen other men following. As they neared, the disciples closed ranks around Jesus.

"Halt!" the young man in the carriage commanded. Those carrying him stopped and set the carriage on the ground. The young man quickly dismounted and ran over to Jesus, kneeling before him.

"Good teacher," he said, his eyes on Jesus' feet.

"Why do you call me good? No one is good—except God."

The man looked up but continued to kneel. "Answer my question, please. What do I have to do to inherit eternal life?"

Jesus smiled. "A very good question." He reached down and helped the young man up. The two of them started walking down the road. The rest of us followed.

"You tell me," Jesus said to him. "What do the Scriptures say?"

"They say, 'Do not commit adultery; do not murder; do not steal; do not bear false witness; honor your father and mother.'"

"Well, there you have it."

"But I've kept all those commands since I was a boy. What am I missing?"

Jesus stopped and looked him in the eye. "You're missing this: go and sell everything you have and give all the money to the poor. And then come and follow me."

The young man looked at Jesus, dumbfounded. His eyes slowly drifted to the ground. He turned away and plodded back to his carriage. His men picked him up and carried him away.

As nighttime fell, Jesus and the disciples continued down the road. *Surely they won't travel very far in the dark*, I figured. And, sure enough, within ten minutes we had come upon a decent-sized town. The disciples stopped at what for this time period passed for a large house. The front door opened, and the owner greeted them warmly. They all entered the house and the door closed behind them.

Great, I thought. *Here I am, stuck at night in a dirty street of some first-century town.* And then it dawned on me: I wasn't really tired at all. I wasn't sure how long I'd been hopping around the first century, but however long it had been, I still had plenty of energy. Unfortunately, I felt quite certain there was nothing to do in this town after dark, and I couldn't exactly open the door everyone had just gone through. Since they couldn't see me, the disciples would think there was a ghost following them.

My problem was solved when the door to the house opened and Jesus emerged.

"Care for a walk?" he said as he passed by me. I turned and joined him.

"Is it safe, walking around this town at night?"

"I wouldn't advise it," he replied.

We took a left and ambled down another dark road.

"That rich man—what did you think of him?" Jesus asked.

"It was sad, seeing him walk off like that." I thought for a moment as we walked. "Why did you just let him go?"

"Because he wasn't ready. He's still hanging on to a false belief."

It felt strange, talking in almost complete darkness. I'd had conversations in the dark before, like on late-night drives, but you could always see the person's face. I could see well enough to tell Jesus was still next to me, but that was about it.

"Which is what?" I asked.

"That this world will provide him with something that will ultimately satisfy. Outwardly, that man is the exact opposite of the woman in Samaria. He has wealth, power, authority, friends, family, faith. He has access to everything this world has to offer. The woman has none of that, but they both are asking the same question. Deep down, they are both asking, *Where's the life?* Because they know they don't have it. The difference is that the woman has already concluded that it is not something this world is going to offer her. The material realm, the temporal realm—it will always leave her thirsty."

"But the rich man hasn't reached that conclusion yet," I added.

Jesus didn't say anything.

"This way," he said after a few moments. We turned to the right and Jesus continued silently. I felt increasingly awkward, not because we were walking in the darkness, but because we both knew what I was thinking. *Am I different from the rich man? And even though I know God, am I still expecting this world to satisfy me?*

I thought about Jason. I was barely handling life without him. I guess it was natural to grieve the loss of a relationship. Nevertheless . . .

"Maybe if I made better choices . . ." I said out loud, mostly to myself.

"Doesn't matter."

"If I'd been more committed . . ."

"Wouldn't have helped."

I turned and stared at Jesus. "What do you mean it wouldn't have helped?"

"None of the things the world offers can be your ultimate source of satisfaction. Relationships, jobs, possessions, traveling, money—you won't find your ultimate satisfaction in the created realm. Neither will the woman at the well. And neither will the rich man. It can't be found there. God hasn't put it there. That's his gift."

"What's his gift?"

"The disappointment. The misery. That everything in the created realm will fail to meet your deepest needs. God designed you for something much more."

"But . . ." I really didn't know what to say. How honest could I be with Jesus? These were things I wasn't usually willing to be honest about even with myself. "But I have a relationship with you already. I mean, I put my trust in you as my Savior a long time ago."

"Yes?"

"And . . . well . . ." I had never admitted this to anyone else, but I felt like my whole life screamed it. "You haven't met my deepest needs either."

I couldn't believe what I had just said. I had just accused Jesus of being inadequate. We rounded a corner, and Jesus walked toward a certain house—maybe the one we started at; it was hard to tell.

"Where are you going?" I asked.

"Inside," he replied without looking back.

"Wait!" I strode after him. "Wait! I'm sorry—"

He turned toward me. "For what?"

"For . . . for what I said. Did I hurt your feelings?" Was that even possible? Did Jesus get his feelings hurt? "Are you mad?"

I couldn't see his face at all. I certainly couldn't read his expression.

"No, Emma," he answered gently.

"Am I coming inside with you?"

"No. You've done what you needed to do here."

"What did I need to do?"

"Admit the truth to yourself."

He opened the door, reached inside, and pulled out an oil lamp that must have been hanging just inside the door. I looked into his eyes. There wasn't any anger in them, or even disappointment. Just compassion.

"So now what do I do?"

"You learn to see things differently. You wondered if the Scriptures were relevant. That was your question, wasn't it?"

"Yes," I said, my head hanging a bit.

"Well, now you'll see."

FIVE

I was standing in a dimly lit room. An oil lamp, gently lighting one corner, cast shadows over the remainder. Near the room's center was a long, low table. Jesus was reclining next to it. I started to speak, but he held his finger to his lips.

I heard a knock on a door behind me and swung around toward it.

"Please come in," Jesus said.

The door opened, and an older man stepped through the doorway. He was sixty, maybe, with a gray mustache and beard. He was dressed in a fancy white robe with gold trim and a red sash around his waist. He wore a white headdress lined with purple and gold. *This guy is no peasant*, I thought. He looked back through the door, as if to make sure no one had seen him enter, and then quickly closed the door behind him.

"Teacher," he said.

"Nicodemus," Jesus replied. "Join me, please."

Nicodemus? I knew that name. Wasn't he a high-ranking Pharisee? That would make sense of his clothing.

The man reclined next to the table opposite Jesus. Jesus reached for a loaf of bread, broke some off, and held it toward him.

"Please," he said.

The older man took it. "Thank you." He took a bite, as did Jesus.

"What brings you here, Nicodemus?"

"Questions," Nicodemus replied. "Questions I'd like answered, if possible. I know you're a teacher who has come from God. If God weren't with you, you couldn't do the miraculous signs you're doing."

"This is how God's Kingdom operates," Jesus answered. "Do you want to know more about the Kingdom?"

Nicodemus nodded.

"Then I tell you this in all earnestness: no one can see God's Kingdom without being born again."

That's what Jesus and Nicodemus talked about— being born again. But why did Jesus want me to hear a conversation about being born again? I was already born again. I had already put my trust in Jesus as my Savior at a summer Young Life camp when I was eleven. I already knew I was going to heaven.

Nicodemus's brow creased. "But how can I be born when I am old? I can't go back inside my mother. I can't be born a second time around!"

Jesus smiled. "What I'm about to tell you is completely true. No one can enter God's Kingdom without being born by the Holy Spirit. People give birth to people. But the Holy Spirit gives birth to spirit. You shouldn't be surprised that I say you must be born again."

Jesus paused before continuing. "It's like the wind, which blows wherever it wants to. You hear the sound it makes, but you don't know where it comes from or where it's going. That's the way it is with everyone born of the Spirit. You see the results, but you don't know how it's happening in them."

There was a knock at the door.

"Come in, please," Jesus said.

A man in simpler clothes opened the door. He looked at Nicodemus. "Teacher," he said to Nicodemus. "Do you have a moment?"

Nicodemus looked at Jesus, clearly not wanting to leave. "I'll be right back," he said. He got up and left with the man.

Jesus pulled another piece of bread from the loaf. "Some bread?"

I took it and had a bite. It was coarse and tasted very plain. *Panera Bread would be a hit in this place*, I thought.

As I finished my bite, my earlier question formed in my mind. "Why did you bring me here? I already know about being born again."

Jesus took another bite before responding. "Yes, you do. But you don't really understand what happened when you were born again. What do you think humanity's main problem is, Emma?"

That was a pretty sweeping question. Poverty. War. The list was endless. I guess underlying all of that was the real answer. "They are sinful," I said. "They need their sins forgiven."

"True, they are sinful. And they do need their sins forgiven. But that's not the main problem."

"It's not?" I replied. Surely, from God's perspective, that was the main problem, wasn't it?

Jesus shook his head. "No. Forgiveness is not the main problem. Not even sins are the main problem. If someone could somehow stop all their sins, they would still have the same problem."

"Which is what?"

"That they are dead."

That's not what I expected to hear.

He continued. "When humanity rebelled against God, people died on the inside. They died to God. Their spirit, the deepest part of them, was completely cut off from God. People are walking corpses. They are physically alive, but the deepest part of them is cut off from the life of God. The problem with a corpse is not that it does bad things. The problem with a corpse is that it has no life."

I thought back to the first few verses of the Gospel of John. I had memorized them long ago, at another Young Life camp. *In him was life, and that life was the light of men.*

"God is life," I said.

"Yes. People are cut off from God. The only solution is for God to birth his life in them. That's what being born again is. It's receiving the life of God. Nicodemus should know this. He's a teacher of Israel. It's right there in the Hebrew Scriptures."

In the Old Testament? "Where?"

"In the prophet Ezekiel, for one. 'I will give you a new heart and put a new spirit in you; I will remove from you your heart of stone and give you a heart of flesh.'"

"It sounds like a heart transplant."

"It *is* a heart transplant. When someone places their trust in me and is born again, God literally takes out the old spirit, dead to God and opposed to him, and in its place gives them a new heart, created in his image, alive to him. The Holy Spirit himself then forever unites himself to that person's new spirit, becoming one with them, giving them God's life. The person they were has ceased to exist. A truly new person has been born."

I thought about that for a moment. "But I'm still a sinner," I objected. "I still sin all the time."

"You still sin, yes. But in the deepest part of your being, in your true identity, you're no longer a sinner. You are one born of God. And God doesn't give birth to sinners."

"Then how come I still sin, if the deepest part of me has been changed?"

He took another bite and offered one to me. I took it to be polite.

"That," he said, "is a lesson for another time. For now, I want you to understand what happened when you entered the Kingdom of God. You didn't just get your sins forgiven. A lot more happened than that. The old you ceased to exist. A new you was created, and I joined myself to that new you. You and I are one. Forever."

He rose and walked around one end of the table. I rose as well. "Where are we going now?"

"I'm going to talk more to Nicodemus when he returns. He needs to understand these things too."

"And what about me?"

"You are going to learn more about how life operates in the Kingdom. That's where you live now."

I hesitated a moment. "I'm not being thrown into another storm, am I?"

He smiled. "If you are, Emma, we will be there together. I'm always with you, remember?"

SIX

I WAS STANDING AT the back of a very large, very quiet crowd on level ground next to a large lake. It was, I assumed, the Sea of Galilee. The people were all looking forward, listening to someone speak. There was no way for me to see the speaker or to move through the crowd to get closer. Not that I really needed to. I knew exactly who it was.

"If someone strikes you on one cheek," I heard him say, "turn the other also. If someone sues you and takes your cloak, don't stop him from taking your tunic, either."

I'd read those words time and again. I'm not sure I'd ever paid all that much attention to them. No one had ever struck me on the cheek or taken my cloak. Granted, I'm sure Jesus' words had broader application, but still, they seemed far removed from my life in Dallas.

"If anyone asks you for something, give it away. And if anyone takes what belongs to you, don't demand it back."

Hardly anyone ever asked me for anything—at least any money—except for junk mail or spam e-mails. And I don't think Jesus had those things in mind.

"The way you want others to treat you—that's how you should treat them. Love your enemies. If people hate you, do good to them. If they curse you, bless them. If they treat you badly, pray for them."

My ears perked up. I had read those words plenty of times before, too. Now they seemed to speak to me personally. I thought about Jason. He wasn't exactly my enemy, but he had hurt me badly. When was the last time I had prayed for him?

"If you love people who love you, what reward are you going to get for that? Even sinners love those who love them. If you do good things to those who do good things to you, what are you doing more than others? Everyone does that. But love your enemies, do good things to them, and lend to them without expecting to get anything back. Then the Most High will reward you greatly, because he is kind to those who are ungrateful and wicked."

The teaching stopped. I had no idea what was happening up front, but gradually the crowd started dissipating. I finally made my way forward. No one even seemed to notice my presence. *Once again, Ms. Invisible.*

As I approached the front of the crowd, Jesus looked my way and our eyes met. He signaled me with his head, as if to say, "Glad you could make it."

I was close to Jesus when four men walked up. I couldn't hear what they said, but their words seemed to trouble Jesus greatly. A look of sadness overcame him. He turned to some of the disciples next to him.

"Get the boats ready to go to the other side of the lake. I need to be alone."

As they tended to three boats on the shore, the last of the crowd went away. Jesus walked over to me. His tone seemed somber. "Are you ready for another boat ride?"

"Depends on if a storm is coming," I replied, smiling.

"Not this time." He didn't seem to be in a joking mood.

He climbed into one of the boats and made his way to the bench in the back. I followed. How, I wondered, would Jesus and I possibly have a conversation in this boat with the disciples in it? Since they couldn't see me, Jesus couldn't exactly sit in the back and be seen talking to himself, could he? Four of the disciples got into our boat. The others got into the other two boats, and we all launched into open water.

My fears, as it turned out, were unfounded. With

the wind, the splashing of oars, and the talking of the other four men, the ride was not the serene trip I had imagined. I waited for Jesus to start the conversation, but he didn't. After we had traveled a ways out onto the lake, I spoke.

"What did those men back there say to you?"

"They told me that John was beheaded."

"John?"

"John the Baptist."

Right. It was easy to forget that, until this point, John had still been alive. "And that bothered you a lot?"

"Yes."

"Because he was a prophet? The one who introduced you, sort of?"

"He was my cousin. But more than anyone else, he was my kindred spirit. Before he was even born, the Holy Spirit was inside him."

"That's why you wanted to get away for a while."

"Yes."

I guess I wasn't prepared to see Jesus affected emotionally by events around him. I think I had always thought of God—of Jesus, too, I guess—as kind of stoic, unmoved by people. That view wasn't accurate, I was discovering.

"I'm sorry if I'm interrupting that."

He smiled gently. "No, it's all right. I arranged it, remember?"

We traveled across the water in silence for a few more moments. The lake was beautiful, actually—deep blue and surrounded by grassy hills. I finally got up the nerve to quietly say what was on my mind.

"What you were teaching back there—that's how life operates in the Kingdom, isn't it?"

"It's part of how it operates."

"But in my situation—how can I even apply that to Jason anymore? I mean, we've broken up."

"Jason isn't the only person in your life."

"But even if we were still together, I'm not sure how well what you were saying would work. I—"

"Love doesn't do what works," Jesus replied.

That's not what I expected to hear. "What does that mean?"

Jesus leaned over the side of the boat, cupped some water in his hand, splashed his face with it, and patted it dry with the outer cloak he had taken off and laid next to him on the bench. He turned to face me. "Emma, love simply loves. It doesn't love to produce a result. Demanding a result is never love. As I said on the beach, God is kind to the ungrateful and the wicked, regardless of whether they respond to his kindness. Being kind means choosing to be good to someone for their benefit. It's not based on how they act. It is doing what's best for the other person regardless of their behavior."

"But isn't there a limit to that?" I objected. "What if you really do get nothing in return?"

"No," he said firmly. "There's no limit. You are not a parent yet. . . ."

"Are you saying I will be?"

He broke a slight smile. "I'm not saying one way or the other. But if you were a parent, you could relate to this more easily. Good parents are kind to their children. Even if the children misbehave, the good parent does what is best for the child. Sometimes that means disciplining them, yes. But that, too, is kindness. It is seeking the other's best, not your own."

"My parents were good at that," I remarked.

"And you will be too." He winked at me. "We must look past people's performance and see their need instead. There's a need behind the way they act. They need to be accepted as they are. Don't demand that they meet your standards. People are weak. They have failings. Kindness accepts that."

Maybe kindness accepted that, but I wasn't sure I could.

"I'll tell you one more thing kindness does. It brings out the best in people. It gives people your undivided attention and affirms that they're important. The world is constantly rejecting. Kindness accepts them and affirms their worth."

Even when we had been together, I hadn't exactly excelled at affirming Jason. Now it was too late.

"Look for people's good qualities. They need warmth, not coldness. Relationships can't be built on coldness. People need someone not to judge, criticize, and blame in an effort to change them. No one responds well to that. Kindness creates an atmosphere where change is possible. So does patience."

I always thought I was moderately patient, at least when it came to not getting irritated too easily. Of course, there was always room to grow. I knew one area where I needed to be more patient: traffic. In the area of Dallas I'd moved to, the traffic was horrible.

"I'm talking about patience with people, not circumstances," Jesus said, as if reading my mind. "Patience with circumstances is a different issue. Patience with people means long-suffering. When you're patient, you're willing to suffer with someone a long time. You extend them grace over and over, waiting for them to change. That's what God does."

"But what if they never change?"

"They may not, Emma. But *you* will. Being patient means giving up control. People are impatient with others because they want to control them. They want to make others do what they want them to do, be what they want them to be. They have an agenda for them. When others don't cooperate with their agenda, people get impatient. Very impatient. Ultimately, patience is an act of surrender."

"Surrender to what?"

"To God. It's turning your agenda, your timetable, over to God and trusting him. The person you want to see change—you realize they are not yours to control. You give them to God and trust he will work his will in them in his time. In the meantime, you just love them. Because God can change people in amazing ways."

I sighed deeply. How life operated in the Kingdom seemed . . . impossible. How could anyone actually live that way?

"Love never fails, Emma. And you have a choice to make. Do you want to succeed, or do you want to fail? Because success in the Kingdom of God and success in the world's eyes are very different. Do you want to operate as one in the Kingdom of God or as someone from the world?"

"Are you saying that God brought Jason into my life to teach me to love?"

"Jason—and everyone else in your life. Relationships are messy. Every one of them provides an opportunity to learn, to grow." He looked out over the lake and seemed to think for a moment. He spoke again. "You don't learn to love by being comfortable, Emma. You don't grow if everything goes your way all the time."

"So pain causes growth?"

"No, it doesn't. But God often uses pain to make you ready to grow. It's up to you whether you cooperate with him. You don't really learn to love unless you are confronted by unloveliness. You don't learn to be patient until someone makes you impatient. You don't learn to forgive deeply unless you are hurt deeply. If you let him, God will take the pain in your life and weave it into beautiful patterns."

"If I let him," I replied.

I had been shutting everything out except my conversation with Jesus. Suddenly I became aware of the sounds of other people—many other people. I looked out ahead of the boat. We were close to the other shore. A large crowd of people awaited us. Word must have spread that Jesus was headed this way. They wanted him to heal them, probably. Or feed them. Or both. Didn't Jesus get tired of a crowd showing up wherever he went?

I looked over at him. He was putting on his outer cloak, getting ready to leave the boat.

"What are you going to do now?" I asked him.

He looked out at the crowd. It was growing. I could see people running toward us from all directions.

"I am going to meet their needs," he said.

"But I thought you wanted to get away from everything for a while."

He nodded. "I did."

SEVEN

THE FIRST THING I noticed was the stench. The smell of dead fish assaulted my nostrils. I was standing on a beach by the Sea of Galilee again. I couldn't see the far side. Grassy hills sloped down to its shores. In front of me were a couple dozen fishing boats tended by fishermen. To my right lay a fishing village with small, adobe-looking houses, all with flat roofs. I didn't see anyone familiar.

I walked into the village. Once again, the towns-people didn't even see me. Being invisible, I had to admit, was kind of cool. But other than being able to talk one-on-one with Jesus, what good was it? What could I possibly want to do in some first-century vil-lage that being invisible would let me do?

I came to an open area in the middle of the town. Some distance away, a man was sitting on a stone ledge and speaking to a gathering of about twenty men.

Another fifteen or so women stood on the edges of the gathering, all with heads covered. I walked closer. I didn't need my eyes to tell me who was speaking. I recognized the voice.

"If someone does something wrong toward you," he was saying, "go and tell him how he wronged you, just between the two of you. If he accepts what you say, you've won him over and restored the relationship. But if he won't listen, take one or two others along, so what they've seen and what they say can convince him."

One of the men standing closest to Jesus asked, "Lord, how many times am I supposed to forgive my brother when he does something wrong toward me? Seven times?"

That's got to be Peter, I thought.

A grin crossed Jesus' face and he laughed. That took me aback. I guess I had never really pictured him laughing.

"I tell you what, Peter," he said. "Don't forgive him seven times. Forgive him seventy times seven times."

Peter's brow furrowed. He looked around at the other men standing there, who seemed just as lost as he was. "Seven times—that's . . . 490 times. Who can keep track—"

Jesus put his arm around him. "No one can keep track of that many times. That's the point." Jesus glanced around the crowd and his eyes settled on me.

"I'm going for a walk," he said to the men around him. "Can you cook some fish?"

He headed straight toward me and nodded in the direction of the beach as he passed me. I followed. In a few moments small waves were lapping close to our footsteps.

"It's good to see you again, Emma."

"At least I'm not getting hit in the face by waves anymore."

He laughed. Laughter seemed to come easily for him. I don't know why, but I never, ever would have pictured Jesus that way.

"What were you laughing about back in the town square?" I asked.

"Peter."

"What about him?"

He smiled and shook his head. "He thought he was going to be commended in front of all those people."

"For what?"

"For being so generous. The rabbis have already answered Peter's question, and he knows it. Three times. That's what they say. You have to forgive someone up to three times."

"And then what?"

He shrugged his shoulders. "And then you can hold a grudge and be bitter, I suppose. Religion is always trying to quantify things. You forgive someone three times, then you can check that off your list of spiritual to-dos. You've fulfilled your quota for God."

"But Peter said seven times."

We stepped over a rivulet of water running down to the lake. "Yes. He took the rabbis' prescription, doubled it, and added one for good measure. Very generous on his part."

"But isn't seven enough?"

"No number is enough. The question is not how often; it is how much. How much are you going to love this person? Love forgives. That's because God is love, and God forgives."

Jesus reached down, grabbed a stone off the beach, and skipped it on the lake. "Back in Jerusalem we talked about being born again."

Is that where we'd been with Nicodemus, in Jerusalem? I had wanted to go to Jerusalem for years, and when I was there, I didn't even know it.

He continued. "And I said it was time to learn how life operates in the Kingdom of God. Remember?"

"Yes."

"Well, here it is. God is love. So what do you think his Kingdom operates on?"

"Love."

"And what does love do?"

"It forgives," I said quietly.

I thought about Jason and me. I had never really

forgiven him for moving on from me so quickly. How could I? Is that really what Jesus expected me to do? It seemed impossible.

Jesus angled left and walked away from the water toward a large piece of driftwood. I was glad for the break in the conversation. I wasn't even sure what to ask about forgiving. He sat on the driftwood and I sat next to him.

"You feel very hurt," he said.

I couldn't help tearing up. The pain was so raw, so close to the surface. "I'm not sure who hurt me more—him or me." We sat silently for a few moments. "I think about him all the time. I hurt all the time. It's like a punch to the stomach every minute of the day." Tears drifted down my cheeks. I stared at the ground through misty eyes.

"Do you want to be whole, Emma?"

I nodded. He didn't say anything. I finally asked, "How do I do that?"

"Here's how you can start," he replied. He picked up a stick and bent down, writing with it in the sand.

Love forgives.

Jesus straightened up and looked at me. "Love doesn't keep a record of wrongs. Love forgives. You have a choice to make, Emma. What are you going to do with what Jason has done toward you?"

"But what does that mean, to forgive Jason? I can't forget what he's done."

"No one is asking you to forget. Forgiving means giving up the right to hold him accountable for the wrong. It means canceling the debt and not holding it against him."

"But how can I possibly do that? It hurts so much." I pushed the tears back.

He nodded. "And you can keep on doing what you've been doing. You can let your hurt harden into bitterness. You can keep your mental record of wrongs and replay it again and again and live in self-pity. You can hold a grudge. You can become cynical and, finally, hateful. All those things will feel good to you, at least for a while. They will seem to balance out your pain."

"And then?"

"Then you reap the consequence."

"Which is?" I wasn't sure I wanted to hear the answer.

"Death. If you live that self-centered way, something's going to die. Something inside of you—your peace, your joy, your compassion for others, your perspective on what's happening. And something outside you—in this case, your ability to be in a truly loving relationship."

I shook my head. "But forgiveness is so hard."

"You think forgiveness is hard? I'll tell you what's

hard—not forgiving. In fact, it'll *make* you hard. Hard-hearted. It will devour you and everything around you. You'll never be at peace."

A slew of questions bombarded my mind. "But what if Jason never shows any remorse?"

"Love forgives."

"But what if I keep on hurting?"

"Love forgives."

"What if he doesn't even want my forgiveness?"

"Love forgives."

Finally I blurted out the biggest question. "But what if I don't want to forgive him?"

Jesus stood up from the driftwood. He picked up his stick and scratched out "Love forgives" in the sand. "Well, that's the real issue, isn't it?"

* * *

I found myself sitting on a mountainside overlooking what I took to be the Mediterranean. The scene was gorgeous. Brilliant blue water stretched to the west as far as I could see. Nearby to the north I could see a city—a Roman city, from what I could tell, with a large amphitheater. White beaches ran to the south.

It was an ideal vacation spot. But people in this century didn't take vacations, I guessed. I wasn't here for one either.

Next to me were my Bible, my journal, my pen, and a handwritten note. It said simply,

Take some time on what we just discussed.

How these things got here . . . well, it didn't matter. I had everything I needed to get started. Except for knowing how to do it.

I opened my Bible and flipped aimlessly through it. *There has to be something in here about how to forgive.* But if there was, I didn't know where to look. I wasn't sure how much I would find on forgiving others in the Old Testament. There was something in the Psalms—no, that was David asking God for forgiveness. The Gospels . . . I had just heard Jesus' teaching right from his own mouth. But he didn't really say much about how to do it. Was there anything in Paul's epistles? There was the "love chapter" that people usually read at weddings—1 Corinthians 13. Did it say anything about how to forgive? I couldn't remember. I turned there and started reading:

> Love is patient, love is kind and is not jealous;
> love does not brag and is not arrogant, does
> not act unbecomingly; it does not seek its
> own, is not provoked, does not take into
> account a wrong suffered, does not rejoice in

unrighteousness, but rejoices with the truth; bears all things, believes all things, hopes all things, endures all things. Love never fails.

I sat back and sighed. *Love may be how God's Kingdom operates, but how can anyone pull this off?* I wasn't too bad at being patient, usually. And I considered myself a fairly kind person. I didn't brag much and certainly didn't think of myself as arrogant. I couldn't remember the last time I acted unbecomingly. *Unless breaking up with Jason in the first place counts.* But not seeking my own? Who could do that? *Everyone* seeks their own.

Maybe I'd been provoked by Jason. My thoughts concerning him our last few weeks together hadn't exactly been magnanimous. As for not taking into account a wrong suffered . . . well, that was why I was on this mountainside, wasn't it?

Forgiveness, Jesus had said, means canceling the debt. Not holding someone responsible for repaying it.

I picked up my journal. I turned past all the pages of the last several weeks—all of the grief and tears that, in the end, never really seemed to resolve anything. On the first blank page I started to write down the things Jason had done wrong to me. If I was going to forgive, I needed to be specific, didn't I?

I wrote and wrote and wrote. I wrote for three

pages. At the end, I wrote in big letters the last and biggest offense:

Moved away from me, and then wouldn't even consider getting back together with me but went looking for someone else immediately, even though I had loved him for two years and he had pledged his love for me.

I put my pen on the ground, tears running down my cheeks. After three pages of preparation, I was more upset and felt even less like forgiving Jason than before. He had run out on me, and then, when I was confused for a couple of weeks, completely dumped me in favor of someone he had just met. I felt utterly betrayed. Everything I had hoped for, everything I had dreamed of for the past two years, had all been flushed down the drain. There he was in Atlanta, moving on with his life, happy and successful, and I was seven hundred miles away, picking up the pieces. Alone. I just couldn't believe he had done this to me!

I closed my journal and stared out toward the sea. The sun, high overhead when I got here, had traveled halfway to the horizon. I wasn't any closer to forgiving Jason than when I'd arrived. Further away, actually. *I suppose there's only one place to go for help.*

I began to pray aloud. "God, I don't know how to forgive Jason. I want to forgive him." I wasn't sure that was true, but I prayed it anyway. "You want me to forgive him. But I don't know how. I don't know how to get past all the hurt. I don't know how . . ."

I started crying again. Maybe my tears would move God to help me get past all the pain and forgive.

I prayed some more. I journaled some more. I resolved to be forgiving. I prayed some more after that. As the sun was about to dip below the sea, I finally gave up. I hadn't really forgiven.

Nevertheless, the last thing I wanted was to spend the night on the mountain alone. I hurried down the mountain to the city below. It was dark by the time I got there. I couldn't believe, on the one hand, how utterly dark it got in the first century and, on the other, how bright the stars were. It had never occurred to me that people in the past had lived each night under a complete blanket of stars.

I stumbled in the dark the last few minutes before finally making my way into the city. *If only I had something to do in this place for the next twelve hours. An all-night coffee shop might be good.*

I found what appeared to be an inn, just to get out of the night air. I crossed the threshold . . . and found myself in broad daylight, on the beach again by the

Sea of Galilee. Jesus was sitting on the same piece of driftwood where we had been talking.

"How . . . how long have I been gone?"

"About a minute," he replied. "How did it go?"

My eyes drifted to the ground and I shook my head. "Not good. I couldn't do it. I couldn't forgive Jason. I just . . . I just don't know how. I know that God's Kingdom operates on love. I feel like . . ." I looked up at him. "I feel like I've completely failed."

"Of course you have." He stood up from the driftwood. "Now we're ready."

"Ready for what?"

"To get on with it."

"With what?"

"God's life."

EIGHT

SUNLIGHT STREAMED THROUGH four open windows. The room I found myself in was large—large enough for a rectangular table in its middle that could probably seat fifteen. *Although people here don't sit at tables. They recline.* The walls looked old and cracked, and nothing hung on them. Apart from the center table, there wasn't anything in the room except a small table on the far side. The door to the room was closed. I was alone.

Standing in the center of the room, I could see out the windows the rooftops of several buildings across the street. I was in a city, on a second floor, I supposed.

I could hear voices outside. Many voices. I walked over, stuck my head out, and looked down at a street market. The air reeked of exposed meat being sold on the street and people smelling like they hadn't bathed in a month. How did people ever live like this?

I turned back into the room and glanced around. Was Jesus planning to meet me here?

Out of the corner of my eye, I saw two items on the table against the wall. I walked over to examine them. One was an inkwell with a primitive reed pen in it. The other was a piece of parchment with writing on it. It was another handwritten note.

Emma,

Take a bit of time to write down the things you need to do when you get back home to work on your spiritual growth. What are the most important activities for you to be doing?

It didn't have a signature. But surely Jesus wrote it. Who else even knew I was here?

I hadn't really given any thought to going back home. But I couldn't pop around the first century forever. This note indicated I'd be going back, maybe fairly soon. Maybe that was why Jesus wanted me to consider my plans for spiritual growth.

I looked once again at the instructions. I picked up the parchment and the pen and inkwell, almost spilling it in the process, and transferred them to the large table. Its top was only a couple of feet off the ground. I reclined. How did people do this every day? It was so uncomfortable—especially for writing. I sat up straight, crossed my legs, and dipped the pen in the ink.

So, what did I need to do when I got back home?

My mind riffled through the usual list of spiritual to-dos. I'd done some of them pretty well and pretty consistently a few years back. During my time with Jason, I had kind of slacked off, but I could get back in the swing of things. I started jotting down some ideas.

More personal Bible study

More prayer

Have a consistent devotional time

Of course, more Bible study and prayer would themselves probably mean a consistent devotional time. But if there was some overlap between these ideas, so what? I started writing again.

Get back to Scripture memory

I wasn't sure I wanted to do that, but it belonged on the list of possibilities, at least.

Listen to the Scriptures

I could listen to some New Testament audio recordings in the car.

Read more books on Christian living

I hadn't exactly read a lot the last couple of years. I hadn't read any Christian books at all, actually.

I looked over the list. All of these were individual things. *What about other Christians? I'm supposed to be doing things with them, too, aren't I?* I jotted down the first thoughts that came to mind.

Attend Bible studies

Join a home group from church

Attend church every Sunday

Find a spiritual mentor or accountability partner

I thought for a few moments. All of these things had to do with my own growth. What about others? What about Christian service?

Find ways to serve others

Take a short-term mission trip

Share my faith

I stopped and glanced over the list. Thirteen items. Surely that was a good start. I hadn't been specific about how I was going to do any of them, but I could worry about that later. And I had left some things off. Fasting, for instance. *Not a big surprise, I suppose.*

I heard a noise across the room. Someone was sliding something under the door—a piece of parchment.

"Hello?" I asked.

I hopped up and walked quickly across the room. I opened the door, but no one was there. I closed the door and picked up the parchment. It was another instruction.

Circle the one that will help you grow the most.

Which one of these things would make me grow the most? I sat back down and looked over the list. All of them were good disciplines, but more than any of the others, one stood out to me. I circled "Have a consistent devotional time."

A knock at the door startled me. I got up and stepped toward the door, then stopped. What was I supposed to do now? No one here could see me except Jesus. If it wasn't him . . . how would they explain a door opening by itself? I concluded that was their problem. I opened the door.

"Emma." It was Jesus. He walked in, closing the door behind him. "Did you finish the test?"

"I didn't know it was a test."

"Of a sort."

He walked over, reclined next to the table, and looked at my list. I sat across the table from him.

"Uh-huh," he said as he read it. He nodded a bit. "Uh-huh." He finished and glanced at me. "Could you pass me that pen and ink?"

I pushed them across the table.

"Thank you. Let's cross out the ones that won't actually make you grow spiritually, shall we?"

"Sure," I replied.

He picked up the pen, dipped it in the ink, and crossed through "Share my faith" at the bottom. I could see his point. Sharing my faith was important, but maybe not the most important thing I could do for spiritual growth.

He crossed through "Take a short-term mission trip." I always thought taking a mission trip would spur my growth quite a bit, but I supposed Jesus knew what he was doing.

He crossed through "Find ways to serve others."

"Isn't serving others important?" I asked.

"Of course. But it won't make you grow spiritually."

He dipped the pen in the ink again and crossed through "Find a spiritual mentor or accountability partner," "Attend church every Sunday," "Join a home group from church," and "Attend Bible studies."

"But wait a second," I objected. "Don't I need to do those things?"

"They are good things," he responded. "But they won't make you grow spiritually."

He dipped the pen once more and looked at the sheet. He crossed through "Read more books on Christian living," "Listen to the Scriptures," and "Get back to Scripture memory."

I could see crossing through the first two— most people through the centuries didn't even have Christian books, let alone Scripture recordings. But Scripture memory? Didn't the Bible say to hide the Word of God in your heart?

Jesus dipped the pen once more. He crossed through "More personal Bible study." He crossed through "More prayer." He crossed through "Have a consistent devotional time." He handed the paper back to me.

"There you go."

I stared at it, dumbfounded.

"None of those things will make you grow spiritually, Emma."

"Then what will?"

NINE

COOL NIGHT AIR ENVELOPED ME. I wrapped my arms around my torso to shield myself from a stiff wind and tried to take in my surroundings. I was sitting on an incline. I could make out the dirt beneath me and some rocks strewn a few feet away. Slowly my eyes adjusted to the darkness. I drew my breath in suddenly as I looked above. The moon and the stars. The half-moon was brighter than I had ever seen it before, and stars filled the sky like infinite points of light on a giant canvas. No wonder our ancestors were fascinated and awed when they looked up at the sky at night. Despite having no idea where I was or what dangers were lurking in the darkness, I couldn't take my eyes off the scene in the heavens.

"This is stunning," I heard myself say.

"Thank you."

I shrieked and whirled around to face the shadow of a man sitting not five feet away from me.

"Jesus?"

"Yes."

I took a deep breath and relaxed as I realized who it was.

"Why did you scare me like that?"

"*I* didn't appear out of nowhere. You did."

I looked around, still unable to make out much of our surroundings. "Where are we?"

"You tell me."

I looked down below as my eyes adjusted more. I could make out a large body of water far below us, the moon shining off its surface.

"Is that the Sea of Galilee?"

"Yes."

The wind blew strongly off the sea against our faces.

"What are you doing up here?"

"Spending time with my Father."

"On the mountain—at night?"

"I must take time to be with him."

I looked back toward the sea.

"Where are the disciples?"

"Down there, trying to row across the sea. They're not going to make it. The wind is contrary."

That was an understatement.

"The winds of this world are always contrary to the children of God," he added. "That's life in a fallen world."

"Did you send them into this wind?"

I looked over at him. I could see the moon shining off his teeth. He was smiling.

"You keep sending the disciples into storms, don't you?"

"Just like I did with you."

I started to reply, but a new thought stopped me. "You're not talking about the storm on the sea when I first appeared here, are you?"

"Not necessarily."

"You're talking about my breakup with Jason."

Jesus didn't respond.

"Are you saying you caused Jason to break up with me?"

"No, he chose to do that."

"So you're saying you made me break up with him first?"

"No, you chose to do that."

I hesitated. "So what are you saying?"

I watched in the dark as he picked up a stone from the ground and tossed it down the hill.

"You have to decide how big your God is, Emma. Is God big enough to take your decisions, made by your free will, and Jason's decisions, made by his free will, and form them into exactly the storm in your life that will accomplish what he wants to accomplish? You have to decide if your God is big enough to trust with every adversity in your life."

Some of the guys in the career group at church were always debating free will and the sovereignty of God. I thought it best just to avoid the debate. Something told me Jesus wasn't looking to debate the matter anyway. I thought through the implications of what Jesus had just said.

"So you're saying the current circumstances of my life are . . . what? 'Ordained by God'?"

"Yes. Absolutely. Just like the disciples right now on the lake. I insisted that they get into the boat and cross over. They were obeying me completely. And heading right into a bad circumstance.

"This is what you must fully accept, Emma. The Father brought you into this circumstance by his will. He will give you grace to endure it. He will teach you what he wants you to learn in it. And by his will, he will bring you out of it again. You are in the sovereign, loving hands of your heavenly Father. He will accomplish his eternally good purposes in your life with complete tenderness."

"Tenderness?" I snorted. "It doesn't feel tender to me."

"Of course not. Suffering never does. But it's the only way."

"The only way to what?"

"To teach you to find your complete life in him. To stop looking for life in things that can't provide it. To give you his very best."

"Which is what?" I asked.

"Himself," Jesus answered. "And if you're going to have all of him, you have a decision to make when the storm hits your life: Do you want relief, or do you want to know the Father? Because the world will never stop offering you quick relief."

I had certainly never thought about my trials—and especially my current trial—that way. "And what if I choose relief?"

"God is patient. Very, very patient. And . . ." He paused. "What you actually find when you seek relief is a good teacher. An excellent teacher."

But not the teacher I want, I thought. "So what you're saying is I need to trust the process."

"No, I'm saying you need to trust a Person. Are you going to trust him in the midst of your pain?" He stood up. "The answer is always a Person, Emma. Always."

He started walking down the mountain. I got up and stumbled after him.

"Where are we going?"

"To the other side of the lake."

"What for?"

"To show you what will make you grow spiritually."

I looked at the outline of the lake in the moonlight. It seemed like a very long walk. "How long will it take?"

"We can take a shortcut."

We descended the mountain. In the dark, I stumbled half the way down. Jesus apparently had more experience traversing mountains in the dark. We stopped at the shoreline.

"Where's the shortcut?" I asked.

"Straight across."

He stepped onto the water and took several steps out on the lake.

"How does that water hold you up?"

"I have no idea. My Father simply told me to walk on it. You can too."

I took a deep breath and then let it out. What did I have to be nervous about? I was still standing on the shore. If this didn't work, the worst that would happen is I'd get wet feet.

I stepped onto the water. Sure enough, it held me up. I giggled and looked at Jesus. "This is unbelievable."

He laughed, turned around, and started walking across the lake. I followed on the water. The night had become darker. Clouds had moved in, obscuring the moon. And the wind was even stronger than before. Despite walking on the water, I was getting drenched by the spray of waves tossed up by the wind.

It took a while, but the novelty of walking on water finally wore off. I was ready to get to the other side, but I had a feeling we weren't even close. This was not a small lake.

Suddenly I heard voices in the darkness ahead and to my right.

"Is that the disciples?" I asked Jesus.

"Yes."

"What are they doing?"

"They're trying as hard as they can to make it across." He kept walking straight ahead.

"And what are you doing?" I asked.

"I'm passing them by."

"Passing them by? Why?"

He stopped on the water. "Because they haven't learned something yet. I gave them instructions, and they think they can fulfill them by their own effort. Their own self-sufficiency." He shook his head. "That's not what this new life is about. It's about dependence—depending completely on a Person. So I'm going to do what my Father always does to the self-sufficient. I'm going to let them have a whack at it. Besides, they're not expecting me to show up in the storm. People rarely look for God in the storm. But that's where they're most likely to find him."

Suddenly I heard a cry from the boat. "It's a ghost! A ghost!"

Jesus turned to me. "See, what did I tell you?" He cupped his hands like a megaphone and called back to them. "Don't be afraid! It's me!"

"Lord, if it's you," I heard Peter shout, "tell me to come to you on the water."

"Come on," Jesus said.

I watched as Peter climbed out of the boat and started walking toward us on the water. After a few seconds he looked around at the waves and began to sink. "Master, save me!"

Jesus looked at me and grinned. As he pulled Peter out of the water, I climbed into the boat. Jesus climbed in with Peter. The minute he did, the boat was at the shore on the other side of the lake.

The disciples looked around in utter shock. So did I. Was that in the Gospel accounts? I'd never heard anyone comment on it. But given what Jesus had just said to me, the meaning couldn't have been clearer. What the disciples couldn't achieve through their own effort was achieved immediately when Jesus intervened. It wasn't about their striving; it was about trust. Was this what Jesus wanted me to know about the spiritual disciplines?

I couldn't escape the implications for my own life.

Jesus disembarked and started walking away from the shore. I joined him.

"Where are we going?"

"I'm going to a nearby village."

"And what about me?"

"There's someone special I want you to see. She will help with the rest of your answer."

As usual, Jesus was one step ahead of me.

TEN

I WAS IN ANOTHER HOUSE, a house with adobe walls and window holes with shutters and a dirt floor. Just like every other one-story house I had been in here. I heard a familiar voice coming from the next room. Jesus'.

I seemed to be in the area where food was prepared. I would have called it a kitchen, except it had not a single thing in common with what I'd call a kitchen. Several women were busy putting together plates of food. They all looked frazzled. One seemed to be in charge, giving instructions to the rest.

I wandered into the main room, where twenty or so people had crowded in. Jesus was sitting in a chair, as were two others. The rest of the guests, including several of the disciples, sat on the floor around the room. Several women sat along a far wall together, along with some children they were trying to keep quiet. One woman, however, sat right at Jesus' feet. She looked out of place there, between the men and Jesus, but she didn't seem to care.

Jesus was teaching, and everyone in the room was listening intently—at least the grown-ups were. I started to as well. I kept trying to match in my mind what he was saying to one of the Gospel accounts, but I couldn't place it. And then I realized that I shouldn't have been the least bit surprised. Most of what Jesus said probably wasn't in the Bible. He taught almost daily for three years, and the Gospel writers only recorded the highlights.

"Kindness and patience are very powerful," Jesus was saying. "But their power may not be evident immediately. It's like this. There was a rich old man who lived alone at the top of a hill. Whenever he came down the hill to the town, he was mean to everyone. So the children used to run up the hill and shout at him, making fun of him. He would come to the door and yell at them, and they would scatter. This went on for a long time.

"But there was one young girl who felt sorry for him. *He reminds me of my grandfather*, she thought. So every week she would pick some flowers from the field, climb the hill, and lay them on the old man's doorstep.

"After a time, the man stopped yelling at the

children, though they still made fun of him. Time passed and the man died. He had no relatives, so the townsfolk had to tend to his possessions. When they entered his house, the girl who had brought him flowers entered as well. She looked at the decorations on his walls in amazement and said, 'He took all the flowers I brought him and wove them into beautiful patterns.'

"On the man's dinner table was a list of the names of all the town's children. By each name was a blessing the man had prayed for the child. At the bottom was a note the man had written. It said, 'When they come of age, please divide my assets among the children of the town. They have been a blessing to me. Apart from their trips up the hill, I would not have learned to love.'"

Jesus was about to speak again, but the woman who had seemed to be in charge in the "kitchen" burst into the room, obviously frazzled.

"Martha," one of the disciples said to her, "is the meal ready?"

She glared at him and strode straight to Jesus, virtually stepping over several guests on the way. Frustration was all over her face.

"Lord!" she exclaimed. "Don't you care that my sister, Mary, has left me to do all the serving alone?"

Martha's statement wasn't exactly true, since she

did have a couple of helpers. But if I'd been in her shoes, I would have felt the same way. Mary was just sitting there, doing nothing.

"Tell her to get off the floor and help me!" Martha demanded.

Jesus looked at Martha, smiled, and spoke gently to her. "Martha, you're worried and bothered about a lot of things. But let me tell you this: only one thing is necessary." He looked down at Mary, who was still at his feet. "Mary has chosen the good part. It won't ever be taken away from her."

Martha looked at Jesus and sighed. What could she say? *I* thought her complaint was justified. She certainly did. But Jesus didn't see it that way at all.

And suddenly, the answer became apparent—the answer to what would make me grow spiritually. I had always thought that the Mary and Martha story taught that we needed to spend more time reading and studying the Bible. And maybe that was true—it probably would be a very good thing for me to do. But I was missing the main point. The main point, I realized, was exactly the same as what Jesus had said to me on the hill overlooking the Sea of Galilee. The answer is always a Person. Mary had chosen Jesus— Jesus *the Person*.

Later that afternoon, Jesus went up on the roof of the house by himself. I took the opportunity to grab a moment alone with him. We both sat down on a small stone wall.

"You answered my question about spiritual growth, didn't you?" I asked him.

He nodded.

"I've always considered what you said to Martha, about what Mary had chosen, in terms of spiritual programs, what I needed to accomplish. But spiritual growth isn't about that, is it?"

He smiled. "The only one who can make you grow spiritually, Emma, who can make you more like me—is me. Spiritual disciplines in themselves have no power to transform you."

"But they do help, don't they?"

"I'm not telling you not to do them. They can be vital. But they only benefit you if they keep you focused on me. On me *personally*, not on me as a concept. Their objective is to keep you at home in me so that you live from the core of who you are—where I am. They aren't to impress people with your spirituality or to mark off a spiritual checklist. They're simply to help you know me, the faithful one who loves you perfectly and acts on your behalf powerfully.

"I am the life, Emma. Only I can live the life in you and through you. And only I can change you into being more and more an expresser of my life. Because that's what you are, Emma. An expresser of my life. I have joined my Spirit to your spirit. I am one with you. We live in total union. And I express myself through you."

I didn't know what to say. That seemed so much more . . . intimate . . . than I had ever imagined Christianity to be. And I was realizing this: that was exactly the way Jesus wanted me to think about my life—as an intimate union with him. That's why he gave himself on the cross, to make that possible.

But a certain question was still nagging me. "Jesus . . ."

"Yes?"

"How can you really say I'm an expresser of you? I'm just a sinner."

He stood up and smiled. "I think we've corrected our share of misconceptions for one day, don't you? Let's save that one for another time."

ELEVEN

WAILING. I was startled by wailing. Not a baby's wailing. Adults' wailing. *Dozens* of adults. The sound made me cringe. What in the world had I come upon?

It was daytime. To my right, in the distance, I could see what must have been Jerusalem, maybe a couple of miles off. To my left I could see a village nearby. The crying arose from there.

Jesus was nowhere in sight. I wanted to hike to Jerusalem, just to get away from the sound of such pain. I'd turned in the direction of the city when I saw several dozen people approaching over a hill. Jesus was leading the way. I immediately recognized some of the disciples behind him.

I waited for him to reach me. Before he did, however, a veiled woman from the village, dressed completely in black, ran to meet him. She was wearing funeral garb. *That must be what the wailing is about.* In some cultures, even in the twenty-first century, loud displays of mourning were how people dealt with death. That's what I'd read, in any case.

The woman had probably been one of the ones wailing, but if so, she had stopped—maybe when someone told her Jesus was approaching.

"Martha," he said as she reached him.

It was the same Martha I had just encountered.

Martha said, "Lord, if you had been here, my brother would still be alive."

Was that an accusation? It sounded like it.

She stifled a sob. "But I know that, even now, whatever you ask of God, he will give you."

"Your brother will be raised from the dead," Jesus replied.

"I know." She sniffled loudly. "On the last day, he will rise again. In the resurrection."

"Martha, *I* am the resurrection. I am the life. Whoever believes in me will continue living, even if he happens to die physically. But everyone who lives and believes in me will never really die. Do you believe this, Martha?"

Martha nodded. She paused a moment before she could get any words out. "Lord, I've always believed . . . that you're the Messiah, the Son of God. The one who comes into the world from God." She turned and hurriedly ran back toward the village. *Why didn't she stay and talk longer with Jesus?* I wondered.

Jesus stayed where he was, surrounded by the disciples. No one said anything. The only sound was the wailing coming from the village. I just wanted it to stop.

In a few minutes another woman dressed in black approached from the village. She didn't run but walked. Her shoulders were slumped. She was the picture of despair. She wept as she walked and was followed by others, both men and women, also weeping. It was Mary. Life for her had changed since I had been at her house.

When she came to Jesus, she fell at his feet. "Lord," she said between sobs, "if you had been here, my brother Lazarus would not have died." Her words were almost the same as Martha's, but the tone was different. She wasn't accusing Jesus of neglecting them. She sounded like she was simply sharing her overwhelming grief about her brother.

And then the thought came to me—is she afraid? She thinks she faces a future without her brother. Lazarus and Martha and Mary lived together. He probably supported the family. Without him, the two sisters were on their own. I imagined the future looked quite bleak to Mary. Or did her trust in Jesus soothe her fears? I didn't know. I couldn't place myself in her shoes.

I looked at Jesus, and for the first time I saw a

troubled expression on his face. He, too, was upset by this scene.

But why? Surely he knows what he's about to do.

"Where have you laid him?" Jesus asked.

One of the mourners said, "Come and see, Lord."

Jesus looked again at Mary, and then he himself fell to his knees. Tears trickled down his face. The tears turned to rivulets, and he started sobbing. I stood there, stunned.

Why was Jesus crying like this? He was, I supposed, sad about his friends being so sad. But I knew he was about to raise Lazarus from the dead. All of this weeping was about to turn into unparalleled rejoicing.

Behind me, I heard some of the mourners who had come from the village.

"Look at how much he loved him!" one of them said.

"This is the man who opened the eyes of the blind," another commented quietly. Nodding heads told me he wasn't the only one thinking that. "If he had come right away, couldn't he have kept this man from dying?"

After a number of minutes, Jesus got up, and they led him to Lazarus's tomb. I had a vague awareness that tombs in first-century Israel were not exactly like twenty-first-century graveyards. That was the truth. The tomb was a cave at the bottom of a large hill of rock. A very large rock—cut for this purpose, I assumed—had been placed at the entrance of the cave.

"Remove the stone," Jesus said.

Martha turned to him, horrified. "Lord, he's been dead four days! By this time the smell will be terrible."

Jesus turned to her and said firmly, "Didn't I tell you, Martha? If you believe, you'll see the glory of God."

Martha hesitated, then turned to one of the men standing nearby. "Remove the stone."

They did so. Jesus looked up to the sky and said, "Father, thank you for hearing me. I know that you always hear me, but I'm saying it now for the sake of the people here, so that they might believe that you've sent me."

He looked toward the tomb and commanded loudly, "Lazarus, come out!"

I held my breath, even though I knew what was going to happen. In a moment, a body wrapped in grave clothes appeared at the entrance of the tomb. Pandemonium broke loose. Several women screamed. Two fainted. One man fell to his knees. Others shouted for joy.

"Unwrap him," Jesus said calmly.

Two men hurried to Lazarus and unwrapped the grave clothes. As they did, another arrived with a robe for him to wear.

I watched for the next several hours as Jesus

celebrated with everyone present, including Lazarus. Needless to say, Lazarus seemed more surprised than anyone that he had emerged from the tomb. Word must have spread quickly; in a fairly short time, the crowd had grown to several hundred people. Around sunset, Jesus dismissed himself from the crowd and took a walk. I joined him.

"You could have prevented all that suffering," I said as we left the village behind, heading toward Jerusalem.

He nodded.

"But you didn't."

"No."

"Why?"

"For the glory of God to be revealed," he answered, and then he paused. "But also for their sake. For Mary and Martha and everyone else here."

I shook my head in confusion. "How was this for Mary and Martha?"

"Because they, like everyone else, were putting all of their faith into a future event. They expect that one day there will be a resurrection and at that time everything will be okay. And that is true, but they were missing the main point."

"Which is what?"

"That God's salvation is *now*. It's present tense. It's not just off in the future. His life is now. *I* am the resurrection, and *I* am life. When I join myself to someone, that's when eternal life begins. Eternal life is not a forever extension added onto your life. Eternal life is a Person. *I am* eternal life. And when I'm living in you, eternal life is living in you. That's present tense. God is always present tense.

"I told you before: I am the life. You don't have any other options for living life the way I created you to live it. I didn't come to help you live 'the Christian life,' as you call it. I came to live my life in you. Because I'm the only one who can do it. Only I can live my life."

We walked in silence for a few moments. I didn't know how to respond. What Jesus had just said was so different from most of what I'd understood from church sermons. No one would put it this way exactly, but I realized the basic message I'd always believed was that living the Christian life was really up to our own effort, with God helping us out when we needed a hand. But Jesus wasn't saying that at all. Why hadn't I gotten this before?

And then a thought occurred to me that stopped me in my tracks. "The lesson at the tomb is the same as it was on the lake with the disciples and at Mary and Martha's house earlier, isn't it?"

Jesus turned around and looked at me. "Why would you think that?"

"Because you said on the lake that the answer is always a Person. And you said at their house that growth isn't about programs and checklists. And that's what you were saying to Mary and Martha today. Their answer isn't a future resurrection. Their answer is *you*."

A smile broke across his face. "Can I quote you on that?"

We laughed.

He glanced up and saw how close we were to Jerusalem. "Let's head back," he said. We turned in the road and started back toward Mary and Martha's village.

"Can I ask you a question?" One had been pressing upon me for several hours.

"Of course."

"Why were you crying before? You knew everything was going to turn out okay."

He didn't answer for a few moments. Finally he said, "I felt such sadness that she felt such grief. I didn't want her to have to suffer so much grief. That was part of it."

Only part of it? "And what was the other part?"

"How horrible, how unnatural, the whole scene was."

"But death is natural," I objected.

He shook his head vigorously. "No, it's not. None of what you saw was as things should be. There is not supposed to be death. People are not meant to live in fear of death. People are not supposed to live lives of destruction, either—the destruction of sin. This fallenness is not humanity's home. Humanity's home is in God. That's what I came to restore."

"Not just in the future?" I asked tentatively. "But now?"

He smiled broadly. "You're starting to get it, Emma."

Night had fallen. The air was now chilly. We stopped on the edge of the village.

"You want to know more about experiencing my life in you," he said.

I nodded. Once again, he was a step ahead of me. "When I go back, how exactly am I supposed to experience this? How do I experience you as the answer?"

"I will teach you, Emma. But you must remember this: it's always by faith. You trust that I am living my life, in you, this very moment. Because that is the reality."

"I'm . . . I'm not sure how to live that out, though."

He smiled. "That's okay. That just means you have to trust me. What is always the answer?"

I grinned at him. "I know."

TWELVE

I WAS INSIDE A HOUSE AT NIGHT. The air was crisp—not the dead of winter in Israel, I guessed, but not summer, either. The smell of food permeated the air. Voices—many voices—arose from the next room. It sounded like a party. I stepped that way and discovered a crowd of thirty, maybe thirty-five people. They were reclining around a table and standing throughout the room, talking and laughing. The windows were shut, and a large fire, along with the heat (and smell) of bodies, warmed the room. The house wasn't built for such a crowd, but that, I had concluded, was the case everywhere Jesus went.

Jesus sat at the far end of the U-shaped table. He was the center of considerable attention, but many conversations were occurring at once. Some of the twelve disciples sat around the table; others were scattered throughout the room. A couple of men were dressed in fancy robes—religious leaders, perhaps. The dress of several others spoke of money. Across the room I saw Lazarus, numerous people crowding around him and eagerly listening to what he had to say.

A woman entered from another room and said something to Jesus. He nodded. She raised her head, and I recognized her. It was Martha. I carefully looked around the room. Someone was missing. Lazarus was here. Martha was here. Where was Mary? I would have expected her to be as close as possible to Jesus.

Jesus looked up and nodded slightly toward me. He didn't appear to be in any hurry to disengage from the party. It looked as if I should settle down for a while. I circled the room and listened. A man named Simon was the host, I discovered. Jesus had healed him of leprosy. We were all in the home of a leper—or a former leper, at least. This was probably the first party he had hosted in, well, maybe ever. He was beaming every second, as if he couldn't get over the wonder of actually having people in his home.

Lazarus was recounting, for probably the thousandth time, what it was like to come out of the tomb. People hung on his every word. Martha circled and served and talked and hummed a tune all at the same time. Several of the disciples were talking about the upcoming Passover. Passover week? I thought back to my years in Bible studies. *Jesus will be crucified soon.*

Sitting across the room, Jesus was just a few days from his death. And he knew it.

Then I noticed something for the first time. Despite all of the talking and laughing, there was a certain edge to the gathering. People kept stealing glances at Jesus and whispering. It was as if the crowd expected something might happen—something not necessarily good.

Several people entering from the next room caught my attention. They brought trays with food and wine. *Lots* of food and wine. A cheer went up from the crowd, and those standing took their seats. Martha was one of the servers, focused on her task yet smiling, enjoying the occasion.

The food was served, and the room grew quieter. Eyes turned to Jesus. He looked up toward heaven and blessed the food. There were smiles all around, and people began to eat. For the first time since arriving in the first century, I was sorry not to be able to join them. *Maybe I could sneak something off a tray*, I thought. Conversations resumed, and pretty soon the room was as noisy as when I had first entered.

One of the guests leaned toward Martha and asked, "Where's your sister?"

Martha shrugged and looked toward the front door. "I thought she would be here by now. She said she had to take care of something."

As if on cue, the front door opened and Mary entered. There was deep feeling etched on her face. She wasn't unhappy, but somber. She carried a beautiful alabaster jar—a vase, really—as though it were worth more than anything on the planet. Her hands trembled slightly. Her eyes focused like a laser on Jesus, as if to her there was no one else in the room. The eyes of a few, then more, then all of the guests turned to her as she moved toward Jesus. She knelt before Jesus at the table and suddenly the room became deathly quiet. I could hear one or two murmurs. "What is she doing?" "Is she bringing him a gift?"

Without a word Mary broke the jar's slender neck. A collective gasp arose as the smell of perfumed oil permeated the room. Breaking the beautiful vase was the last thing anyone expected, until what happened next. Mary rose, stood above Jesus, and poured the entire contents of the bottle—all of the precious oil— over Jesus' head. It ran in great rivulets down the sides of his face and his hair, down his neck, into and under his robe, all the way to his feet. I glanced at the guests. They were utterly stunned. Even the disciples looked astonished.

And then Mary did what I had never seen a woman in Israel do. She took off her head covering and began unbraiding her hair. Jaws all over the room dropped.

One of the men in fancy clothes stood up, crossed the room, and left. The room was completely silent.

Mary finished unbraiding her hair, let it fall down her back, and knelt at Jesus' feet. Then she did the utterly unthinkable. She took her hair in her hands and started wiping Jesus' feet with the oil that covered them. As she did, she wept, her tears mingling with the oil.

Murmuring erupted throughout the room. "Oh, my." "I can't believe what I'm seeing." "That was spikenard. Do you know how much that was worth?" Three more guests got up and left.

Suddenly a man I recognized as one of the disciples stood up and looked right at Jesus, his face filled with rage. "How dare you let her waste that on you! That much could have been sold for an entire year's worth of wages. How many poor people could have been fed and clothed with that, Jesus?"

The attack was infectious. "Absolutely," one of the other disciples said. "That's right," two others chimed in. Many others around the table were nodding.

I looked at Mary. The words had no effect on her at all. She continued weeping and wiping Jesus' feet. Then some of the disciples aimed their reproof directly at her.

"Mary, what were you thinking? How could you be so extravagant?" one of them reprimanded.

"How could you be so wasteful?" another scolded. "Why can't you be practical for once, Mary?"

At that point Jesus stood. He glanced down at Mary, who did not stop what she was doing. He looked at the disciples sternly and spoke quietly but firmly. "Silence. All of you." The room fell silent. "Leave Mary alone. She's doing a wonderful thing—something that never occurred to the rest of you. She gets it. She has anointed my body in advance of my burial. I've been telling you about this for a year. The time is here. She's done a good thing, and you call it evil? She's done a faithful thing, and you call it wasteful?"

He turned to the disciple who started the attacks. He was still standing and was obviously upset. "Judas," Jesus said to him, "you can do good to the poor anytime you want. You always have the poor available. You don't always have me. Mary understands what's going on here. Do you?"

Judas glared at Jesus for a moment, then grabbed his bag and strode to the door and out of the house.

Jesus turned to the other disciples and looked at them one by one. "Do you understand? Do you? Do you? Mary understands more than all of you put together. Everywhere the story of the good news I bring goes, the story of what she's done here will be told as well."

No one said a word. No one moved. Everyone was

looking at the floor. Finally Simon, the host, said, "Well, let's finish the meal, shall we?"

The meal was finished quickly and with little conversation. Mary finally stood up and went into the other room, perhaps to eat there. Guests started leaving the minute they finished eating. Soon it was just Jesus, his disciples, Mary, Martha, Lazarus, and Simon. And me.

In a minute Jesus excused himself, saying he was going to be alone and would rejoin the disciples at Mary and Martha and Lazarus's house. I slipped out the door behind him. A couple of minutes later we were walking along the road to Jerusalem, the moon and stars our only light. As usual, it was a situation I normally would not have felt comfortable in, but I figured I was perfectly safe with Jesus.

"What did you learn tonight, Emma?"

It was hard to know where to start. I, along with everyone else, was a bit stunned by the evening's events. *Is the lesson that it's okay to pour oil over Jesus a few days before he gets crucified?* That didn't seem to have much broader application.

"I'm not sure," I replied honestly.

"Then I'll help you. We all have a story that we tell ourselves about our lives, don't we?"

"Yes, I suppose."

"You always need to take your story and see how

it matches up with God's story for your life. To the degree it doesn't match, you're off track."

"That makes sense." Duh. How could anything Jesus said not make sense?

"Tonight you saw three life stories on display."

I thought for a moment. "You mean Mary's?"

"Yes."

I hesitated. "And Judas's?"

"Yes."

"And . . . " I wasn't sure about the last one. "And who else?"

"The other disciples."

I stumbled over something in the road and caught myself before I fell.

"Watch out," he said.

"Right."

He continued. "A Judas story is a life that tries to use God for its own self-interested purposes. He wants to force God into his story. He's so wrapped up in himself and in what he wants that he can't even form the question, 'What am I willing to be for God?' But I won't accommodate Judas. I'm not here to make his story come true. He finally realizes that."

"So . . . so he's gone to sell you out."

"Yes."

That was sobering. Truly sobering. While Jesus and I were having a nice evening conversation, Judas was already on his way to the religious leaders to betray Jesus.

"Many people have the same story as Judas. They are completely for themselves, and they are only interested in God to the extent he is useful to them. Judas criticized Mary for wasting money. He has wasted his entire life."

"I don't want to tell myself a Judas story."

I could see Jesus smiling in the moonlight. "No. I'm not concerned that you will tell yourself a Judas story, Emma. Your heart is far from that."

That was reassuring.

"You could tell yourself a Mary story. Mary has found someone worthy of unreservedly giving her whole life to. Her devotion is like my Father's love: lavish. She is completely unself-conscious in her extravagant worship. She is so grateful for what God has done for her that she takes the container of her life and pours love out everywhere she goes. No price is too high for her to pay, even if to the world it appears to be utter foolishness. She is willing to spend and be spent for me. Her life is now compelled by the love of the Father."

"I want to have that kind of story," I said.

I saw him nodding. "I know you do, Emma."

He looked back toward Bethany, from where we had come, and we both turned to head back.

We walked a few moments in silence. I asked, "What is the third story?"

"The story the other disciples are telling themselves right now. It was on full display tonight."

"How do you mean?"

"The disciples, too, thought Mary was being wasteful. They didn't get angry about it like Judas did, but they are judging by worldly standards. They want to serve God, but it's still on their own terms. They don't want anyone going too overboard about serving him. They want to serve God when it's comfortable, and convenient, and understandable, and predictable. Right now, they only want to go partway. They don't think that's true, but they are about to discover otherwise. They want to be successful by the world's standards, not the standards of the Kingdom of God. They still think and calculate by the world's standards. They want a Messiah who is, in a sense, safe to follow, who doesn't require much sacrifice."

"But haven't they sacrificed a lot to follow you?" I objected.

"Yes, but not everything. That's the difference between them and Mary. She loves me extravagantly, no matter what it looks like to others. She's never, ever halfhearted about me. She's given herself fully, and the result is what you see: Utter love. Complete joy. Abundant life.

"It's very easy to live in the kind of story the disciples are telling themselves. Be practical. Don't go overboard. God has his proper place in life, but so do other things.

"My Father isn't looking for practical worshipers. He's looking for extravagant worshipers. He's looking for lavish lovers of God. He's looking for people who are willing to be broken and poured out for God and for others, without regard for themselves. Those are the kind of people my life will flow through like a gushing river."

In our last encounter, I had told Jesus I wanted to understand more about experiencing his life in me. "This is what your life in me looks like, isn't it?"

He nodded.

I couldn't help mentally examining my own life and posing the question, *Which story am I telling myself right now?* I wasn't sure I liked the answer. Finally I said, "So God wants me to be more committed, right?"

Jesus shook his head. "No, Emma. He's not looking for more commitment."

I was shocked. How could Jesus say God wasn't looking for more commitment? "So what is he looking for?"

"More abandonment. More complete trust in him. The answer is always a Person, remember? He wants you to know him as a Person, not as a set of religious duties. When you do, you will love him completely and want to do his will fully because you will know his perfect heart of love. And when you know his love, Emma—do you remember what I said to the Samaritan woman at the well?"

"You said she would never thirst again."

"Exactly."

THIRTEEN

I KNEW THIS ROOM. I had been here before in the daytime with Jesus, with the nasty-smelling street market one story below. During the day, its sounds filled the room. Now it was night, and no sounds came from outside, yet the room was noisy with conversation. There was the table at which Jesus and I had sat, talking about spiritual disciplines. Jesus and all of the disciples reclined at it now, their silhouettes flickering on the walls in the eerily dim light of oil lamps.

My eyes drifted over the table. Plates had scraps of food on them. Wine cups were half full. Mostly eaten bread pieces lay scattered. The meal had already been eaten. And then it occurred to me—an upstairs room, Jesus with only his disciples, bread and wine. *This must be the Last Supper, and I just missed it!*

A couple of disciples, still with bread pieces in their hands, started conversing heatedly. I hovered closer. They were arguing about . . . who would be greatest in the Kingdom. Here? I knew they'd had that argument, but at the Last Supper? Jesus had just told them he wouldn't eat this meal with them again until he ate it with them in heaven, hadn't he? He had just said he was going to die, hadn't he? And now they were arguing about who was the greatest? I couldn't believe it.

Several more disciples joined in the argument until it seemed as if the entire room was erupting. Peter finally stood and shouted, "Enough!" Everyone stared, speechless. Peter turned to Jesus. "Master?"

Jesus took a piece of bread, dipped it in oil, and had a bite. He swallowed and looked around at all of them. "The earth's kings lord it over their subjects. People in charge of even minor things love to show off their power. With you, things don't work this way. With you, the greatest must become like the youngest and the leader like a servant. Who's greater in the world's eyes, the one who reclines at the table to eat or the one who serves him? Isn't it the one who reclines to eat? But I'm among you as the one who serves."

At that point Jesus rose from the table, took off his outer robe, and wrapped a towel around his waist. Then he poured water into a basin that was sitting by the wall, and he began to kneel in front of the disciples, one by one, and wash their feet, drying them with the towel wrapped around him. Even in the dim light I could tell their feet were filthy. After three pairs of feet had been washed, the water looked black. Jesus changed it out and continued.

I watched the disciples' faces closely as he washed each of them. I don't think they knew how to respond. Only Judas's attitude was clear. He looked as if he couldn't wait to dash for the door.

Jesus finally came to Peter, who had folded his feet back under himself. "Lord, you're not going to wash my feet, are you?"

"You don't understand what I'm doing now, Peter, but later you will."

Peter shrank back. "No, Lord. You're never going to wash my feet!"

"Peter, if I don't wash you, you don't have any part with me."

Peter immediately stuck his feet and hands toward Jesus. "Then don't just wash my feet—wash my hands and my head, too."

Jesus smiled. "Didn't you bathe this morning, Peter? If you've already bathed, you're still clean, except your feet are covered with dust from the road." He looked around at the disciples. "So once your feet are washed again, you are clean—but not all of you."

Finishing all twelve of them took time. It seemed like an hour. When he was done, Jesus put his robe back on and reclined at the table once more. "Do you understand what I just did? You call me Teacher and Lord. Well said. So if I am your Lord and Teacher and I washed your feet, you ought to wash one another's feet as well. I'm giving you an example so you will do for one another as I have just done for you. Remember: a slave isn't greater than his master. The one sent to do a task isn't greater than the one who sends him. Now that you know this"—he looked around at each one—"you'll be blessed if you do it."

It was a magnificent scene. And then I thought about what Jesus had done. Here was God the Son, humbling himself by doing the dirtiest of jobs on behalf of eleven men who would abandon him—and one who was about to betray him. And I couldn't even bring myself to forgive Jason. How was I ever going to live like Jesus lived?

* * *

I counted only eleven disciples. I knew which one was missing.

I was walking behind them, Jesus at the head, down Jerusalem's empty night streets. Only the disciples' torches and the occasional flicker of an oil lamp through a window lit the stone path. The group walked in silence. I had never encountered them so subdued.

We passed through the gate leading past Jerusalem's

outer wall and followed the road into a valley. On the far side, in the moonlight, I could see the shape of a large ridge. We left the road and walked into an area with small trees. No, not trees. Vines. We were in a vineyard.

Jesus stopped and turned to the disciples. "These vines illustrate exactly what I've been telling you tonight." He reached out and lifted up a vine. "You can think of it like this. I'm the true vine. My Father is the one who takes care of the vineyard. He makes sure the vine is healthy and grows as it should. I'm the vine. Every branch in me that doesn't bear fruit, he takes away. Those branches that do bear fruit . . ."

He looked at one of the disciples. "Thaddaeus, do you have your knife?"

Thaddaeus handed him a small one. Jesus took the knife and cut back one of the branches. "Those branches he prunes so that they may bear more fruit. That's what my Father is looking for—branches that will bear fruit. In your case, what I've been teaching you all this time together has already pruned you. It's made you ready to bear fruit."

I heard an owl hooting in the distance. Other than that, the night was quiet. Eerily quiet.

Jesus handed the knife back to Thaddaeus and then looked around at them all. "Here's what you will need to know: remain in me. That's it. Remain in me. I will remain in you. As I said back at the house, the day is not far off when you're going to know without a doubt that I'm in you and you're in me. This is what you will need to do: just remain in me."

He reached out to the vine again and lifted up a single branch coming out of it. "By itself, this branch can't bear fruit. We all know that." He picked up a small branch, not more than a twig, really, lying by itself on the ground. "Do you think this thing can produce a grape?"

I looked around at the disciples. Normally, one of them, Peter probably, would have immediately answered even a rhetorical question. But not tonight. They were silent, just listening.

Jesus continued. "The only way one of these branches can produce fruit is if it remains in the vine. That's the way it is with you. The only way you can produce fruit is if you remain in me. It's like the night you were rowing against the wind on the lake. How much headway did your own efforts produce?"

One of them answered this time. "None."

"Right. Your own efforts produced nothing. That's the way it will always be now. Your own efforts will never produce anything. They won't produce lasting fruit for the Father."

Jesus glanced down the road as if he knew it was time to move along. He had an appointment to keep. A very difficult appointment.

"Here's what I want you to really remember. I'm the vine. You're the branches. If you simply remain in me, and I am in you—if you do that, you will bear fruit. A whole lot of fruit. But on your own, apart from me, you can't do a thing."

And then I realized something—the answer to the question I had posed for myself at the Last Supper, after Jesus had washed the disciples' feet. I was never going to live like Jesus lived. I was never going to be able to love that way. Not through my own efforts, anyway. I couldn't produce that kind of life on my own. That's what Jesus had just told the disciples. Apart from him I couldn't do anything.

But Jesus living in me . . .

FOURTEEN

It wasn't night, but neither was it day. The sky was darker than the darkest clouds could make it. It seemed as if time itself had been suspended in this place.

I stood outside the high stone walls of Jerusalem. People were walking up the road from the city, traveling in hushed tones and glancing around anxiously, as if they didn't know what to make of the earth that day. Their attention seemed to be drawn to something behind me. I turned and looked, but I was not prepared for what I saw.

On a hill directly in front of me stood three tall, wooden crosses. A man was hanging on each, wrists and feet nailed to the wood with large metal stakes. All were naked. To take a breath, each agonizingly rose on their nailed feet. Above the head of the man in the middle a sign had been posted: JESUS THE NAZARENE, THE KING OF THE JEWS.

Roman soldiers stood nearby. So did many others, including men in fancy robes and headwear hurling insults at Jesus. Several women knelt near the foot of the cross, weeping.

My gaze quickly returned to the source of their sorrow. I had heard people talk before about Jesus on the cross, but all the words disappeared when I was confronted with the real thing. I felt as if my heart would break as I looked at him—thorns pressed into his head, blood running in streams from his head and back. His face was so beaten it was barely recognizable as human.

And then, as I looked, the scene changed. Or, rather, it didn't change; it came more into view. I was seeing . . . I wasn't sure, exactly. Was I seeing more than the physical realm? Was it a vision?

Whatever I was seeing, its impact on me was immediate, and I cringed in horror at what I saw. I had heard sermons about the physical torture of the cross. But suddenly I realized that the physical reality, as horrible as it was, wasn't the worst of what was happening. Surrounding Jesus was a terrible, living blackness, as if all evil had gathered to torment him. Demonic beings of unfathomable ugliness and hate hovered around his head, mocking him and howling in delight. I turned my face away in revulsion.

"Look!" someone next to me said.

I turned and saw a man looking right at me. How could he see me? No one else in this century could except Jesus. I stared at the man. There was something different about him . . . something like the rest of what I was seeing. And then it dawned on me: he wasn't a man. He was an angel.

"Look!" he repeated.

A light emanating from above grabbed my attention. I looked back toward the cross. A piercing, pure light fell on it from the sky as another angel slowly descended. In one hand he was carrying several pages of parchment. In the other he was carrying a hammer and a nail. The demons howled at the sight of him, but they parted as he approached. He slowed, circled the cross once, then alighted on its top. With one stroke of his hand he nailed the parchment to the cross, above Jesus' head.

"What is that?" I asked the angel next to me.

"It is your certificate of debt to God, his righteous decrees against you because of your sins."

The other angel flew back into the sky. My gaze returned to the cross. It was as if I was seeing with new eyes, and my heart could barely contain what I saw.

I was seeing into Jesus—not his body, but his spirit. And what I saw was a holiness, a purity, a love so overwhelming in its brightness that I almost had to turn away. *In him was life, and that life was the light of men,*

John had written. I was seeing that light in all its glory, and it was too much to bear. Words from the book of Revelation came back to me: *He was like the sun shining in its full strength.* My brain shouted to turn away, that my eyes could not endure the vision, but I remained, transfixed.

Then something changed. The brightness dimmed, then dissipated entirely. It was being replaced by something—an invisible weight descending on the hill. I didn't see it at first. I felt it, a great, oppressive heaviness, from where and consisting of what I didn't know. All I knew was that every fiber of my being told me to run from it. Then it began to appear, hovering above the cross—an evil so loathsome, an emptiness so overpowering that I heard myself screaming, "No!"

It hovered above Jesus, and I watched, horrified, as it enveloped him. Then I saw the exchange. Where I had seen Jesus' spirit, now I saw only the dreadful, grotesque evil. Jesus himself had somehow become the evil of the world. And I knew in my heart that this was the most horrific thing that had ever happened. That *could* ever happen.

I turned away again. The physical torture was difficult enough to witness, but what was happening in the spiritual realm was unbearable.

"Look!" the angel next to me said again.

I lifted my eyes, and I was confused. Suddenly Jesus

was not alone on the cross. Another being began to appear there, hanging with him. At first it looked like an apparition, but it became increasingly solid as the seconds passed. As it solidified, I saw it possessed an empty darkness, a void so gruesome I could barely continue holding it in my sight. It was missing something vital, the absence of which made its being unspeakably tragic. Somehow, I realized that everything about the being was for itself; its existence was defined by its own self-interest.

As the being came more clearly into view, it became superimposed over Jesus, neither one shielding the other from view, but both hanging simultaneously on the cross. Finally I could make out the features on the other being's face. I stared unbelievingly at it.

It was me.

Suddenly Jesus cried from the cross, "My God! My God! Why have you forsaken me?" The demons screamed with unbridled delight and fury at him. I heard Jesus say, "Father, into your hands I commit my spirit." He cried out with a loud voice and died.

I thought my heart would explode because of my love at that moment for him, for what he had endured for me. Then my attention was drawn to the other being on the cross—to me. And as I looked, I realized that the me on the cross was hanging there dead, just as Jesus was.

I stood, stunned. Finally I looked at the angel next to me. He looked just as stunned as I was.

"What just happened?" I asked.

"The Son . . . the Son . . . he . . . is dead."

I looked back to the cross. "And what about the other figure I saw there? What about . . . me?"

His eyes didn't wander from Jesus. He didn't answer for a moment. Then he said, in a hushed tone, "He took you there with him."

I tried to let that sink in, but it didn't make any sense. "But I didn't die," I said quietly. "I'm standing right here."

He didn't respond. Without looking at me, he added, "He joined you to himself. He took the old you, your old self, opposed to God"—he turned to me—"and he crucified it." His eyes returned to the cross, and he stared in wonderment. "He crucified it."

I looked back to the cross, to Jesus hanging there, lifeless. "What happens next?"

He shook his head slowly. "I do not know."

FIFTEEN

I FOUND MYSELF IN a garden filled with trees. On two sides, natural rock walls formed its borders. Cut into one of the walls was a cave entrance. It reminded me of the entrance to Lazarus's tomb. As with Lazarus's tomb, off to the side, there was a large boulder to cover the entrance. Here, it hadn't been rolled into place yet.

Or . . .

"Emma."

Startled, I turned and looked behind me. It was Jesus! He was marvelously alive. I immediately felt like hugging him, but I was too self-conscious to do that. I simply stepped toward him and said, "It's so good to see you."

"It's good to see you, too, Emma."

He nodded toward the entrance to the cave and we walked to it, ducking to go inside. The cave's roof was low, maybe five feet. On the far side was a bench—a slab, really. Some white cloths had been rolled up and left on it. There wasn't any doubt in my mind where we were.

"This was your tomb."

"Yes."

And that slab was where they put his body.

"What happened while you were in here—from Friday afternoon until Sunday morning?"

"What needed to be done, was done."

Something told me I wasn't going to get any more details than that. Jesus crossed to the bench and sat on one side of it. I sat on the other.

"I wish I could have been here when you were resurrected."

He smiled warmly. "You *were* here, Emma."

I looked at him, not understanding.

"Remember what you saw on the cross?"

I thought about my vision. I had been joined to Jesus on the cross. I had died with him there. The Bible said I died with him, was buried with him, and was raised with him.

"Dying and being raised with you—that isn't just metaphorical, is it?"

He shook his head. "Hardly."

"I really did die on the cross. And I really was raised with you."

He nodded. "Do you understand now why what

you said about being 'just a sinner' was wrong? In fact, Emma, you aren't a sinner at all."

Before witnessing the cross, that statement would have seemed completely out of bounds. But now the realization of what had happened there, and here in the tomb, was dawning on me.

"Because the old me, the sinful me, was put to death with you on the cross." In my vision, I had seen the horror of the sinful me that had been joined to Christ.

"Yes."

"And here"—I glanced around at the rock walls of the tomb—"a new me was raised with you."

I could see the pleasure on his face at what I was coming to understand. "Because God does not give birth to sinful offspring, Emma. The new you, the person you are now in the depths of your being, was created with my own nature. And, as I said before, I have joined myself to it—forever."

I sat back in amazement. I really was a new creation in Christ. God actually had performed a heart transplant. The old me was gone. I was someone entirely new.

But then a troubling thought intruded. "So if I am a new creation, why do I still sin?"

He smiled warmly. "Well, that is the logical question, isn't it?"

He motioned toward the entrance of the tomb. "Let's go for a walk, okay? This place is a bit confining."

He rose from the slab and I did the same, hitting my head on the roof of the cave. "Ow!"

"Careful."

He led us out of the cave, through the garden, and onto a dirt road. I could see the city walls behind us as we walked away. Behind the city, sunlight was just appearing over the hills. It was early in the morning.

Early in the morning . . .

"What day is this?" I asked.

"Sunday."

"Sunday . . . the Sunday you were—"

He laughed. "No. The next Sunday. I was very busy last Sunday."

That was the truth.

We rounded a bend in the road and came upon a hill. I recognized it immediately. The crosses had been taken down, but the location was etched in my memory. Calvary. A week before, Jesus had been crucified here. The area was deserted. We walked to the bottom of the hill and stood silently. I wasn't sure exactly what to say.

"Thank you for what you did here," I finally said.

He answered quietly. "You're welcome, Emma." He walked slowly around the bottom of the hill and looked up at the top again. Then he turned to me. "Do you understand fully why there can't be any condemnation of you now?"

I thought about the scene I had witnessed at the cross. "You died for my sins. You took the punishment."

He nodded. "It was all laid on me. There is nothing left to punish. My Father doesn't deal with you according to your sins, Emma. The sin issue has been completely taken care of."

He walked slowly up the hill and I followed. "There was another thing that happened."

An image came to my mind. "The decrees against me. That's what the angel said when the other angel nailed something to the top of the cross. That it was the decrees against me, my certificate of debt to God."

We got to the top of the hill. I looked down at the holes where the crosses had been placed.

"Yes," he responded. "God's righteous judgments against you were nailed to the cross. There can be no more judgments against you. No more accusations. No more having to make up any debt. You've been set free from that forever."

He turned and looked out over the valley toward the city, and then back at me. "One more thing happened here. The old you, your old spirit being, dead to God—the sinner, the rebel, the enemy of God—was executed here. Just as much as I was."

And then it was evident to me. "There's no one left to condemn, is there? That person has already been killed."

A smile broke over his face.

He looked toward a ridge that led to another hill a long stone's throw away. "Let's go over there." We walked along the ridge and sat down at the top of the nearby hill. In the distance, toward Jerusalem, I could see people beginning to fill up the road leading into the city.

"So you haven't answered my question yet," I said. "If I'm a new creation, why do I still sin?"

"That's simple," he responded. "Your inner being has been born of the Spirit. But you still live in a body—with a physical brain—that hasn't been set free yet. One day you'll have a new body, and who you already are will become completely evident to the whole universe. In the depths of your being, you are already on the same page with me. You love the Father. You want to do his will. You want to glorify him. But there's a power in your mortal body that keeps pulling you down. One day, that will be gone. For now, you live in an in-between time."

"But how do I live in this in-between time? I'm always failing. How am I supposed to—"

He held up an index finger and I stopped. "You're asking the wrong question, Emma. The question is not *how*. The question is *who*. Remember what the answer always is?"

"A Person."

"Right. You can't deliver yourself from your dilemma. Only I can. That's why I've come to live in you, to live my life through you. I'm not asking you to try harder to deliver yourself. Just the opposite. I'm telling you to stop trying. Instead, start abiding."

When Jesus had been teaching the disciples about abiding, I'd had a realization. I wasn't able to produce Christ's kind of life in me. Only he could do that. Still . . .

"I guess I'm not sure what it means to abide."

Jesus stood. "Let's walk back toward the city."

We walked down the hill and got back on the road to Jerusalem. We passed several people on the road, who, as usual, didn't seem to see me. But the more people we passed, the more it became evident to me: they saw Jesus, but none of them recognized him. You'd think *someone* would. It was like those two disciples on the road to Emmaus after Jesus had been resurrected. They didn't recognize him either.

"Abiding isn't complicated," Jesus said. "Actually, it's a very simple thing. It's like in that vineyard over there." He pointed to our left.

"We don't have to go back to the vineyard to talk about this, do we?"

He laughed. "Not unless you want to. In any case, one of those branches over there doesn't have to strive to remain in the vine, does it?"

"No."

"No. It's already in the vine. And the vine is in it. It only has to remain where it already is. That's the way it is with abiding. How much effort do you put into breathing?"

"Not much. I just do it."

"Right. You just do it. Abiding is that simple. It's the most natural thing in the world for a child of God."

"Then why does it seem so hard?"

"It's not usually hard at all. But there's a discipline to it. It's not a discipline of self-effort, though. It's a discipline of consistently choosing."

"I thought all disciplines were self-effort."

"Self-effort doesn't produce fruit. Remember the disciples rowing against the wind on the lake? Apart from me you can do nothing."

"Then what is it about?"

"It's about loving attentiveness to God. Or, to put it another way, it's about staying home in me. It's the most natural thing in the world for the branch to stay at home in the vine." He stopped and picked up a stick along the road. With it, he drew a picture of a simple house in the dirt. "A house is where you live. It's your home. It doesn't take a lot of effort to stay home. It's where you already are. Your home is in me. You simply remain there. You do that by being lovingly attentive to me.

"Everything you need to live is in your home, isn't it? Food, clothing, and so forth. It's the same with me. Everything you need for life is in me, because I am the life. Except unlike your physical home, my life never needs to be replenished. It's always sufficient. It's always abundant. It's always overflowing.

"In your home in me, you have everything you need. All the love. All the strength. All the forgiveness. It doesn't come from you. It's mine, and I live it in you. You give your life to me, abandon yourself to me, trust that I am lovingly, sovereignly arranging every circumstance in your life for your good and the good of others, and guess what comes?"

"What?" I asked.

"Peace. Peace like you haven't ever had. Joy. Love. Knowing you are loved, and being able to give that love away. You walk into a room and you don't really like anyone there—what do you want to do?"

"Leave."

"Yes. That's your soul's reaction to the situation, and it's fine to have that reaction. That's being human. But guess what being lovingly attentive to God would look like?"

I thought for a moment about what he'd been saying. "I guess . . . it would mean saying, 'God, what do you want to do here?'"

"Yes! It's letting every situation, every circumstance,

every reaction you have escort you back to the Father. And back to me. You say, 'Jesus, I feel like leaving, but you are in me to love. Is there someone here you want to love through me? I can't do it, but you are my perfect supply. You can do it through me.' You do that, and you watch the love flow through you."

He put the stick down, and we started walking again.

"Branches aren't expected to produce anything on their own," he said. "They can't. Neither can you. Stop trying."

"But how? I have to try to live the Christian life, don't I?"

"No, you don't. And you never will as long as you're trying to. This is all about dependence. You depend on me for everything. As you depend on me, as you trust in me, then as you step out in faith, you will find that I am your strength. I am your love. I am your devotion."

We passed a person walking a donkey along the road and fell silent. "Let me give you a few secrets about abiding," Jesus said when we were out of earshot.

"I thought there weren't any how-tos about this."

He laughed. "Well, they aren't how-tos, really. They're just ways of cooperating. I'm still the only one who can produce the fruit. So for starters, don't demand understanding. Rather, follow the Spirit's lead."

"But I thought we were supposed to understand things, at least what God's will is."

"Yes, understand the Father's will. Absolutely. Just don't demand to understand why, or how it will work out, or whether things will go the way you want them to if you obey, or any of that. Just obey immediately what the Spirit is telling you. Obedience leads to understanding. It almost never works the other way around."

I thought for a moment about what Jesus just said. "To obey someone without understanding first requires trust."

He nodded. "You're absolutely right. I want you to learn to trust me completely. Abiding means abandoning yourself to me. It's saying, 'Lord, you can do what you want in my life, through my life, and I'm going to trust you. Even if it takes me through heartbreaking trials, I'm going to trust your loving heart to cause every event in my life to work for my good and your eternally good purposes."

We walked silently for a minute. I couldn't help thinking through the implications of what Jesus had just said. I was still in the middle of a heartbreaking trial. Was I willing to trust God's goodness and sovereignty to cause even this to work together for good?

Jesus finally spoke again. "Here's another part of the same truth. Give thanks for everything. Praise my Father for everything."

"But I don't *feel* thankful for everything," I objected.

"I didn't say *feel thankful*. I said *give thanks*. Praise God. It's the ultimate expression of faith to thank and praise God for what hurts you, especially when you can't see how things will ever work for good. When you give thanks despite what you may feel, you will begin to know my Father, and his love for you, much more deeply."

We passed a garden on our right. It wasn't the garden with the tomb. It was . . .

"Is that the garden of Gethsemane?" I asked.

"Yes."

Jesus started walking that way. In a few moments we were among the trees where he spent that last, awful night.

"Do you remember what I told the disciples about my death? I called it my Father's cup. I told them it was the cup my Father had given me to drink. I could have seen it as coming from Judas, or the religious leaders, or Pontius Pilate, or the Roman soldiers, or the crowd who called for it."

He shook his head gently. "But no. They were the human agents, but nothing happened to me that my Father didn't ordain. It was *his* cup for me, and his alone. And though the suffering was great, what that suffering produced was far, far greater."

We stopped underneath a large tree. Jesus turned

toward me. "Everyone who is mine will have such trials in their life—suffering that the Father uses for good."

I thought about what he had just said and about my own life the past several months. "Jason is the Father's cup for me, isn't he?"

"Yes, he is."

Tears drifted down my cheeks. Harder and harder they fell, until the trees around us disappeared in the haze of my tears and all I could see was the pain. Then I felt two arms encircling me and holding me tight. I stood, crying, and Jesus stood, holding me, for what seemed like an eternity. And somehow, in the grip of his embrace, the pain melted into a different sensation . . . that of being loved. In the midst of it all, I had been, and was being, and would be loved.

After many minutes we parted. Jesus wiped the last tears from my eyes. And then I noticed something that surprised me. There were tears in his eyes too. We smiled at each other.

"The Father wants me to see that cup as coming from him."

"Yes."

I thought for a moment about what Jesus had said just a bit earlier. "He wants it to bear great fruit in my life."

Jesus nodded. "But whether it does is up to you. You can choose to see it as coming from Jason only and grow bitter. Or you can see it as your Father's goodness—his gift toward you—and let it usher you into a deeper experience of my love, my presence, and my life in you than you've ever imagined."

I looked around the garden. What Jesus had gone through here was horrific, as was the cross. But there was an end to the suffering.

"There really will be an end to the suffering and God's joy in the morning, won't there be?"

"Yes, Emma. There will be."

I looked back at the city, which I could see through the trees. "This is the end of my time here, isn't it?"

"It is."

I thought about how I got here—the card, the pantry door. It seemed like so long ago. "Something tells me I won't be walking through any more open doors. At least, they won't bring me back here."

"You don't need them anymore, Emma. You have an open heart now."

I turned to him. "I'm not completely sure I can do the things you've taught me. Not without you standing next to me."

He smiled gently. "You already have a Teacher. He will teach you everything you need to know. And I will live through you everything that needs to be lived. It's my life, remember? Just remain in me."

I looked at the ground in front of me, then back at him. "So how do I get back?"

"I will send you myself. But first I want to give you an assignment. You can call it your first lesson."

"Lesson in what?"

"In being lovingly attentive."

We walked out of the garden and toward the city. Jesus talked, and I listened.

My APARTMENT LOOKED exactly the same as when I left it. The pile of mail on the kitchen table, my Bible on the coffee table next to the couch, the ice cream sandwich wrapper on the kitchen counter. I glanced at the clock. 6:23. Hadn't it been 6:23 when I left? I hadn't been gone a minute!

I walked over and picked up the greeting card. It read the same:

For a real adventure with Jesus, go through the nearest open door.

And there was still no signature. But at the bottom, where a signature might have gone, eight words had been added in the same handwriting. They said simply,

I in you, and you in me. Forever.

151

I couldn't help but smile.

I looked around the apartment. I still missed Jason. And it would take a little time to get used to not being with Jesus in person.

"But thank you, Father," I said—not with a lot of confidence, but I said it. "This is your cup for me now. You are teaching me to trust and to be attentive to you."

Then I remembered the lesson Jesus had taught me as we walked back toward Jerusalem. And I realized there would never be a better time to obey immediately than now.

I bowed my head and said, "Abba—"

Jesus had said to me, "Don't address him as God. He *is* God, but he is much closer to you than that. He is your Father. But he is even closer. He is your Abba, as little children here call their fathers. The Holy Spirit has been sent into your heart, and guess what he cries out in you? 'Abba!'"

So I bowed my head and said, "Abba, thank you for this cup you've given me. It really hurts, but I choose to believe you are working your loving, eternal, good purposes in me through it."

I paused for a second. As I said that, for a couple of seconds I actually felt the reality of it. God *was* working my circumstances together for my good. And then I remembered something else Jesus said. "Forget your feelings. They will come and go. It's great when you have good ones. To trust, you must choose, not feel."

I bowed again. "Jesus, I can't do this myself. But you've made me a new creation. You've made me a forgiver. And you are the life in me now. So I choose to forgive Jason. I don't feel like it, but I choose it. I've been crucified with you, and it's no longer I who live, but you living in me. So it's not just I who forgive. You forgive in me. And Jason, whom I now forgive, I forgive by your forgiveness, Jesus. You love me and gave yourself for me."

I looked up and felt . . . nothing. I didn't feel a wave of forgiving emotions. I didn't feel any magical release from the pain of the breakup with Jason. It seemed as if nothing had changed. I had simply done what Jesus told me to do.

My phone beeped on the table next to me. My friend Allison from my old church had sent me a text:

Hey girl. Just read a paraphrase of a verse that spoke to me and u came to mind. Hope u r well. John 14:21: "The person who does what I tell him to do is the one who really loves me. To him I will reveal myself, and show him how much the Father and I love him."

And then I knew. I was on a real adventure with Jesus.

Online Discussion *guide*

TAKE *your* TYNDALE READING EXPERIENCE *to the* NEXT LEVEL

A FREE discussion guide for this book is available at bookclubhub.net, perfect for sparking conversations in your book group or for digging deeper into the text on your own.

www.bookclubhub.net

You'll also find free discussion guides for other Tyndale books, e-newsletters, e-mail devotionals, virtual book tours, and more!